EDITOR: LEE JOHNSON

  WARRIOR SERIES

SARACEN FARIS
1050–1250 AD

Text by
DAVID NICOLLE PhD
Colour plates by
CHRISTA HOOK

First published in Great Britain in 1994 by
Osprey, an imprint of Reed Consumer Books Ltd.
Michelin House, 81 Fulham Road, London SW3 6RB
and Auckland, Melbourne, Singapore and Toronto

© Copyright 1994 Reed International Books Ltd.

All rights reserved. Apart from any fair dealing for the purpose of private study, research, criticism or review, as permitted under the Copyright, Designs and Patents Act, 1988, no part of this publication may be reproduced, stored in a retrieval system, or transmitted in any form or by any means, electronic, electrical, chemical, mechanical, optical, photocopying, recording or otherwise, without the prior permission of the copyright owner. Enquiries should be addressed to the Publishers.

ISBN 1 85532 453 9

Filmset in Great Britain by Keyspools Ltd
Printed through Bookbuilders Ltd, Hong Kong

Dedication
For Umar Leslie Hegedus and Khadijah Knight, who also strive for Islam.

Publisher's note
Readers may wish to study this title in conjunction with the following Osprey publications:
MAA 171 *Saladin & the Saracens*
MAA 75 *Armies of the Crusades*
MAA 155 *Knights of Christ*
MAA 105 *The Mongols*
MAA 259 *The Mamluks*
Elite 9 *The Normans*
Elite 19 *The Crusades*
Campaign 19 *Hattin 1187*

Artist's note
Readers may care to note that the original paintings from which the colour plates in this book were prepared are available for private sale. All reproduction copyright whatsoever is retained by the publisher. All enquiries should be addressed to:
Scorpio Gallery
P.O. Box 475
Hailsham
E. Sussex BN27 2SL
The publishers regret that they can enter into no correspondence upon this matter.

For a catalogue of all books published by Osprey Military please write to:
The Marketing Manager,
Consumer Catalogue Department,
Osprey Publishing Ltd,
Michelin House, 81 Fulham Road,
London SW3 6RB

SARACEN FARIS AD 1050-1250

INTRODUCTION

Soldiers of slave origin were the elites of most Islamic armies from the 11th–13th century but never formed a majority; the bulk of Muslim troops were free men. The professional cavalryman was generally known as a *faris* or 'horseman' in Arabic, a word that carried overtones similar to – though not identical with – the Western European knight. The dates chosen for this book also require some explanation. The European Crusades of the 12th and 13th centuries were transitory incursions of marginal importance to Middle Eastern history. Much more significant were the Saljuq Turkish invasion of the mid-11th century and the devastating Mongol assault of the mid-13th century. These Central Asian eruptions similarly had greater impact on Middle Eastern armies.

CHRONOLOGY

1029	Ghuzz Turks invade eastern Iran.
1055	Saljuq Turks conquer Baghdad.
1086	Saljuq Sultan replaces Arab princes of Iraq and Syria with Turkish governors.
1092–6	Saljuq civil wars.
1095	Byzantine Empire appeals to Pope for help against Saljuqs.
1097–9	First Crusade invades Anatolia and Syria; Crusaders capture Jerusalem.
1101	Crusading armies defeated by Saljuqs of Rum (Anatolia).
1101–8	Saljuq civil wars and rebellions.
1115	Saljuqs defeated by Crusaders at battle of Danith.
1122	Caliph of Baghdad raises independent Abbasid army.

Two camel-riders in Bedouin Arab costume in a late 13th century Syrian copy of the Maqamat *of al Hariri. (British Lib., Ms. OR 9718, f.173r, London)*

1127–8	Zangi appointed governor of Mosul; Zangi takes control of Aleppo.	1190–2	Third Crusade retakes Acre; fails to reconquer Jerusalem.
1144	Zangi of Mosul retakes Crusader-held Edessa (Urfa).	1193	Death of Saladin; start of fragmentation of his (Ayyubid) empire.
1146	Nur al Din succeeds Zangi in Aleppo.	1194	Last Saljuqs of Iran overthrown by Khwarazmians.
1148	Second Crusade defeated outside Damascus.	1218–21	Fifth Crusade invades Egypt and is defeated.
1153	Crusaders conquer Fatimid Ascalon.	1220–2	Mongols invade Transoxania, Iran and Afghanistan, and defeat Khwarazmians.
1154	Nur al Din takes control of Damascus.		
1156	Death of last Great Saljuq Sultan; fragmentation of Saljuq Empire.	1243	Mongols defeat Saljuqs of Rum (Anatolia) at battle of Köse Dag.
1163–69	Five Crusader invasions of Fatimid Egypt.	1244	Jerusalem falls to freebooting Khwarazmian army.
1169	Saladin becomes governor of Egypt under Nur al Din.	1245	Ayyubid Empire reunited.
		1249–50	Defeat of St. Louis' Crusade against Egypt; overthrow of Ayyubid dynasty in Egypt; start of Mamluk rule.
1174	Death of Nur al Din; Saladin takes control of Damascus.		
1175	Saladin defeats Zangids (successors of Nur al Din) at battle of Hama.	1256–8	Mongols invade Iran and Iraq and sack Baghdad.
1182–6	Saladin takes control of Aleppo and Mosul.	1260	Mongols invade Syria; defeated by Mamluks at battle of 'Ayn Jalut.
1187	Saladin destroys army of Crusader states at battle of Hattin; reconquers Jerusalem.	1291	Mamluks destroy remnants of Crusader Kingdom of Jerusalem.

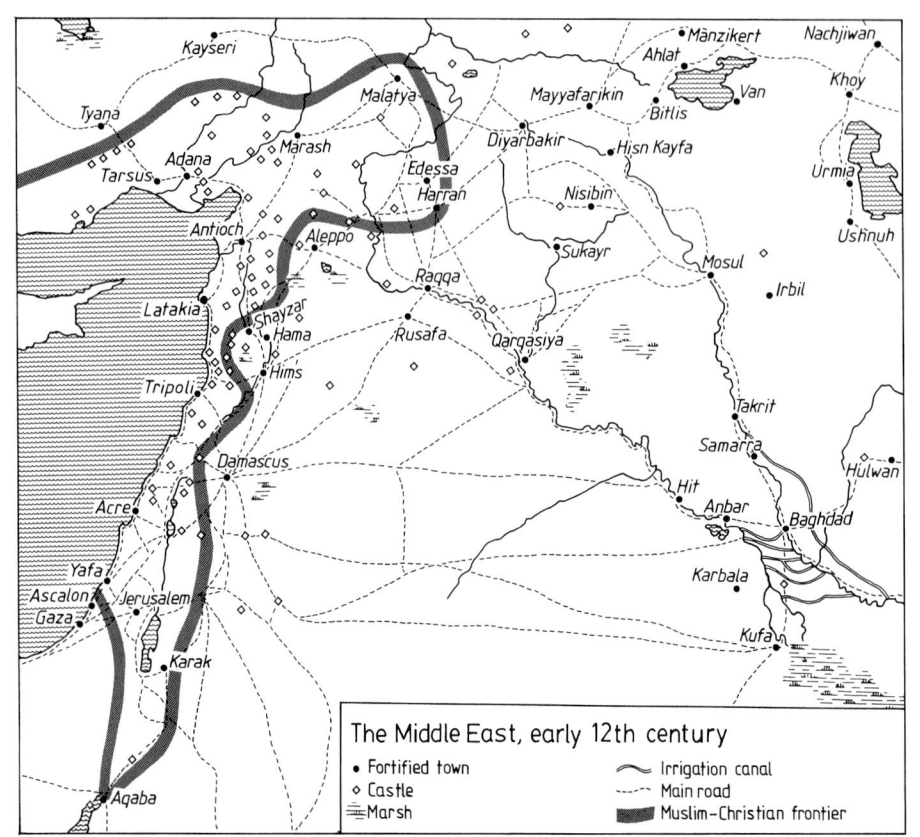

Right: Sgraffito-ware bowl showing a horseman in urban Arab costume, with a hunting bird on his wrist, 13th century (bowl from the Crimea, probably northern Syrian). (State Hermitage Museum, St. Petersburg, Russia)

ORIGINS AND RECRUITMENT

It is in the nature of medieval history that much more is known about the upper echelons of societies and armies than about the ordinary soldiers. Yet this is slightly less true of Islamic civilisation than of Christian Europe. Many leaders rose from the ranks, and some even founded ruling dynasties. Muslim culture, particularly in the 11th and 12th centuries, was one that recognised individual merit and respected the luck or 'divine favour' that enabled a man to win fame, fortune or power. At the same time, a soldier's ethnic or tribal origins could both open and close doors of opportunity.

The defeat of the Arab leader al Basasiri by the Saljuq sultan Tughril in 1059 marked the end of Arab dominance in Syria and the rest of the Fertile Crescent until the area regained independence after the Second World War. The Fatimid Caliphate of Egypt was degenerating into a military dictatorship, and by the time the First Crusade appeared on the scene at the end of the 11th century, the rival Saljuq Turkish empire was crumbling: several areas had been devastated; fortifications were in decay; some towns had been virtually deserted; whole provinces were infested with bandits; and most local Turkish governors were little more than tribal leaders. Yet the threat from Western European Crusades, and later from Mongols, meant that the first priority of each state was to maintain an effective army.

Under such circumstances a military career had obvious advantages. An elite of *mamluk* soldiers, purchased as slaves, trained and then freed, were extremely expensive, and although a ruler's *'askar* or personal regiment might consist of *mamluks*, the rest were normally mercenaries or *jund* soldiers who served for pay, pensions or grants of land. Middle Eastern military and civilian elites had been separate for several centuries and most soldiers were now recruited from the geographical and social fringes. They also retained a distinctive appearance, often reflecting their ethnic origins. The Turks wore long plaits similar to modern Rastafarian 'dreadlocks', and in Yemen many men wore their hair long, as the pre-Islamic Arabs had done. However, in most of the Muslim world men shaved their heads; long hair and extravagant moustaches being the mark of a professional warrior.

Individual city-folk did enlist, though most known examples come from the 10th century. One wealthy young man from Baghdad, for example, had ruined his reputation with drinking and music and so bought military equipment, two horses and two mules, grew his hair, learned to speak and behave like a mountaineer, ate garlic to give himself the required bad breath and served as a soldier for several years. Another account tells of a freed Greek slave who married his master's widow and enlisted as an elite soldier, but after suffering a snake-bite, he cut off his military moustache and retired as a religious ascetic. Early in the 12th century the famous Arab soldier and writer Usama Ibn Munqidh tried to persuade his tutor to become a soldier and fight the invading Crusaders, but the old scholar refused on the grounds that he was temperamentally unsuited.

Rough Turkish and Kurdish warriors were, in fact, tolerated as a necessary evil by the cultured Arab townsfolk of Syria and Iraq. Little information survives about ordinary soldiers and it is misleading to judge the ethnic composition of an army by its senior officers who tended to be Turkish or Kurdish.

A strong sense of group identity, or *sinf*,

The Citadel and town of Shayzar in central Syria. (Author's photograph)

certainly existed among soldiers, often based on tribal origins. The sons of soldiers were still enlisted by some rulers, but were regarded as second best to men from peripheral tribal areas.

Arabs were proud of their reputation as hard-riding light cavalry able to endure greater hardship than most other troops; they dominated warfare in the real desert regions. Most wars were not, however, fought in deserts, but in the fertile cultivated parts of the Middle East, and usually for control of the rich trading cities. The tribal Arabs who served in the Ghaznavid armies of Afghanistan and north-west India were described as 'dare-devil riders', and as vital auxiliary cavalry in the Fertile Crescent (from Palestine through Syria and Iraq to the Persian Gulf).

The fortress-city of Shayzar in Syria remained an island of Arab-ruled territory with a largely Arab army. However, the main employer of Syrian Arab cavalry was the Fatimid Caliphate of Egypt. This service was also well paid.

Closely associated with Arab soldiers were the 12th century *mawali* or 'clients'. Little is known about their origins, and although they attached themselves to a particular Arab tribe, their status was less than that of a warrior born into the tribe.

Like the majority of lowland Bedouin Arabs, the mountain Kurds practised transhumance, migrating along fixed paths according to the season. Like the Arabs their military elites fought as cavalry, being known as 'rough jousters' riding 'shaven' horses, but whereas the Arab's typical weapon was the lance, the Kurds were known as swordsmen. The period of greatest opportunity for a Kurdish soldier was, naturally enough, under Saladin and his Ayyubid successors, who were themselves of Kurdish origin. Kurds offered themselves as individual mercenaries or came as tribal units which would then fight in distinct battlefield units.

Militarily much more important were the Turks, whether free Turcomans, detribalised Turkish professional soldiers or *mamluks* of slave origin. From early Islamic times the Turks had enjoyed a reputation as extremely effective warriors, and there were *Hadiths* or 'pious sayings' to support this: *'I have an army in the east which I call Turk. I set them upon any people who kindle My wrath.'* One early 12th century Arab poet described the Turks as demons in war, angels in peace. They were also famed as archers, for their eyesight and as armourers. But while Turcoman nomads were regarded as good soldiers, they were thought unruly, insisting on prompt payment of their wages, eager for a quick battle and unsuited to patient campaigning.

Armenians played a small, though significant,

military role in the Muslim armies of the 11th and 12th centuries, despite being Christian. They were particularly prominent in Egypt, where part of the Armenian military elite and their families had emigrated after their homeland had been occupied by Byzantine Greeks and then by Turks. Armenian regiments served the Fatimid Caliphs loyally, and when they were finally disbanded by Saladin some individual soldiers migrated south to Christian Nubia where they joined a failed invasion of southern Egypt in 1172. Today it might seem strange that the Christian Armenians fought so enthusiastically for a Shi'ite Muslim ruler like the Fatimid Caliph. However, like the Nubians and the Coptic majority within Egypt, they were Monophysite Christians and as such were regarded as doomed heretics by Greek Orthodox Byzantines and Catholic Crusaders.

The time when Berber soldiers could find guaranteed employment in the Middle East had passed; the Fatimid army had disbanded most of its Berber cavalry back in 1093, though some were still on strength, mostly from western Libya. At the same time, the majority of black African soldiers in the Fatimid army were of slave origin and fought as infantry, though there were also freely enlisted Nubians, Ethiopians and Arab Bedouin from the south.

Clearly a soldier had many potential employers to choose from and men often served in several armies during their careers. Their choice would have been influenced by various factors: the wealth of an employer, religious affiliation and the employer's preference for a particular ethnic group. However, the most important factor was whether other members of a soldier's family or tribe had already served with this or that employer.

All these considerations had an impact on the size of the medieval Muslim army in which the recruit found employment. Some historians still suggest that, unlike Crusader leaders, Muslim rulers could always recruit more armies because of their huge manpower resources but this view fails to take account of the way in which armies were enlisted and the limited populations from which soldiers were drawn. The *Memoires of Usama Ibn Munqidh* shed considerable light on the origins of leaders, officers and lower ranks in one small late 11th/early 12th century army (see table A), although the statistics must be treated with extreme caution.

The recruitment policies of Turkish armies could also vary. According to a Jewish description of a Turcoman attack on Fatimid Egypt in the mid-11th century, the invaders included Turks, Armenians, Arabs, Greeks, various other Anatolians and even 'Germans' (probably meaning Europeans). The Saljuqs and their protégés enlisted Kurds and Daylamite mountaineers, though tribal Turcomans formed the bulk of their armies. As the Great Saljuq Empire fragmented, ethnically varied regional armies reappeared. The troops of previous Arab or Kurdish rulers may already have been absorbed into city militias, yet their descendants were still able to operate as regular soldiers.

The army of Turkish-ruled Damascus was both more important and more typical than that of Arab Shayzar. Here an individual soldier's career

Table A: Ethnic composition of army of Shayzar, late 11th/early 12th century

Rank	Origin of recruits
Governors, military leaders and senior officers (Shayzar and neighbouring states)	Arabs 18.4%, Kurds 5.2%, Turks 73.6% and slaves 2.6%.
Cavalry and junior officers (largely Shayzar)	Arabs 44.4%, Kurds 41.6%, Turks 5.5%, slaves 5.5%, Christian Kurds 2.7%.
Unspecified soldiers including infantry volunteers (largely Shayzar)	Arabs 50%, Kurds 21.4%, Turks 0%, slaves and 14.3%, North Africans 14.3% (plus unspecified 'other North Africans').

Interior of the Bab Antakya (Antioch Gate) in Aleppo, mid-13th century, looking down the Suq al Atarin – once the main street of the city. (Author's photograph)

opportunities were certainly influenced by his ethnic background. Early 12th century Damascus was a military state dedicated to *jihad* against the invading Europeans. Its army consisted of Turks, Kurds, Arab Bedouin, urban militia and religious volunteers. Turks were most numerous, providing military leadership and guard units. The majority came from tribes in the Diyarbakir region of what is now south-eastern Turkey. The rulers of Damascus maintained close links with the region's local leaders and the men could be ordered to Syria if a Crusader threat loomed. A separate group – known as Turcomans rather than Turks – came from the same area but were strictly volunteers who came of their own free will if the Crusaders threatened Damascus. Whereas Turks lived within the city, these Turcomans camped outside. The Kurds of Damascus included cavalry but never numbered more than a few hundred under a single Kurdish officer. Arabs are rarely mentioned in the regular army but frequently appeared on campaign, generally in logistical support.

The most successful among the small armies that emerged from the fragmenting Saljuq empire was that of Zangi and his son Nur al Din. Its leadership was Turkish and Kurdish; the troops were mainly Turcoman horse-archers and Kurdish close-combat cavalry. Most were professional *tawashi* cavalrymen, and they were backed up by Bedouin Arab auxiliaries. It is worth noting that the muster-roll of a large Zangid army in Mosul in 1175 only included 6,000–6,500 cavalry. After Saladin united Egypt, Syria and the Jazira region, he could recruit larger armies than had been seen for many years. The bulk of these were freely recruited professionals, both officers and other ranks, and they were mostly Turks, with the Kurds being of secondary status and importance.

The last time an Abbasid Caliph had had his own army was back in the 10th century, and the reappearance of a small but effective Caliphal army in the 1120s provided potential recruits with another employer. It also offered a military role to those whose religious convictions made them happier to serve the nominal head of 'orthodox' Sunni Islam rather than a 'heretical' Shi'ite Fatimid Caliph or a secular leader whose commitment to Islam was only skin-deep. The revived Abbasid army was largely commanded by Turkish officers. It included Turkish soldiers but by 1193/4 it was mostly recruited from Iraqi Arab tribes and northern Kurds.

TRAINING

Military standards had fallen by the mid-11th century, and the period of the Crusades was one in which Middle Eastern Muslim armies struggled to regain their lost professionalism and high morale. Even so, it is clear that traditions of training, battlefield control and tactics were – in theory if not in practice – far in advance of those seen in Europe.

The basic military skills of a *faris* were known as *furusiya*, a concept which also contained aspects of 'chivalry'. (Mere courage was known as *shuja'a*.) In the 9th century such skills included vaulting onto a horse's back without using stirrups, general riding ability, polo, archery at static and moving targets, and presumably the use of other weapons.

The military elite of the Crusader period were also expected to practise their skills constantly. Late 13th or early 14th century books on *furusiya* list the qualities required of a professional *faris* as: obedience to a superior officer; an ability to make correct military decisions; steadiness in adversity; horsemanship; nimbleness in attack; possession of good quality weapons and armour; and skill in their use. By then *furusiya* exercises reflected the Muslim military elite's traditional willingness to learn from any source, some exercises having come from Khurasan in eastern Iran, others from Byzantium, and a few from the Crusaders. They dealt with archery, use of the lance, sword and mace, wrestling, parade-ground skills, hunting, crossbow-shooting, polo and horse-racing. Many of these 'games', as they were known, were much closer to the British War Office Cavalry Training Manual of 1907 than to the knightly skills being learned in medieval Europe. A professional *faris* was also trained to fight on foot. A quote from one manual shows that the military elite saw the importance of both cavalry and infantry, unlike the European knight who was prejudiced against infantry warfare: *'In some ways the horseman is superior to the infantry, in some ways the infantry is superior, and in other ways they are equal. But for strength of weapons, speed and striking power, if not for care and caution, in feigned retreat or in pursuit, the horseman is superior.'*

Whereas Fatimid cavalry largely fought with spear and sword, the first wave of Saljuq Turkish invaders relied on Central Asian horse-archery tactics of dispersal and harassment. Within two generations the Saljuq professional cavalry, though not the Turcoman tribal warriors, had largely reverted to a long-established Middle Eastern tradition of horse-archery, in which men shot volleys as close-packed units, often at rest. This system needed fewer spare horses and permitted the use of heavier armour. By the 12th and 13th centuries it seems that even in strongly Turkish areas like Azarbayjan and Anatolia the professional cavalry elite relied as much on spears, swords, maces and javelins as on archery.

The Muslim world had a long tradition of military theory, with writings dating back to the 8th century. Most of that written before the 12th century was for senior officers, and it sheds interesting light on military priorities. Greater emphasis was given to foot soldiers than cavalry, and the greatest of all to infantry archers. The counter-Crusades prompted a wave of new military textbooks; some were purely theoretical, others dealt with *jihad*, army administration, broad strat-

Drawing on paper, from Fatimid Egypt, 11th/12th century. On the left a clean-shaven Turk in cavalry boots has a sabre hung from a belt with officer's pendants. On the right a turbaned Arab or Berber with a spear, sash and shoes wears a mail hauberk beneath his tunic. (Museum of Islamic Art, inv. 13703, Cairo, Egypt)

egy, narrow tactical considerations, specific skills or simply with military equipment. Some were apparently aimed at junior officers as well as commanders, and it is clear that high professional skills allied with extreme caution, avoidance of unnecessary casualties and a preference for wearing down a foe without resort to a major battle influenced the training and attitudes of ordinary soldiers.

According to an ideal system described in the *Siyasat Nama*, it took eight years to train a *mamluk* soldier. Although the reality was probably less, the Muslim military elite does seem to have been older – rank-for-rank – than their Crusader foes. The schedule in the *Siyasat Nama* indicates training on foot first, then horsemanship followed by archery. After that a young soldier was allowed 'decorated' equipment. Later still he was entrusted with increasingly important duties.

The reality of training in Fatimid Egypt, at least where elite professional cavalry were concerned, was remarkably similar to the *furusiya* system of the later Mamluk Sultanate. Fatimid *hujra* barracks also served as training centres, and it is possible that here, as in the better recorded barracks of 10th century Tarsus, retired warriors supervised the training of young soldiers. Cavalry skills focused on fighting horsemen and infantry, the use of and resistance to various weapons, striking different parts of the enemy and his horse, and ways of deceiving a foe. *Furusiya* exercises normally took place in a *maydan* or 'parade ground' which was also used as a camping area for an enlarged garrison or army. Larger cities, like Cairo, Aleppo and Damascus, had at least two *maydans*.

The Arab style of riding was closer to that of the Romans than that of the Central Asian Turks: it put great emphasis on long-distance endurance. The riding skills of professional soldiers were probably better than those of nomads, and the 'High Islamic School of Riding', which reached its peak in 12th–13th century Egypt and Andalusia, was an amalgamation of Mediterranean and Persian methods. Here the rider used a saddle and 'seat' similar to that of modern horsemen. This was less tiring for himself and his horse than the riding style seen in medieval Europe. Books on horsemanship showed that a young horseman first learned to ride bareback, to develop a really firm 'seat', and only then was allowed to use a wooden-framed saddle. He had his stirrups set further forward than in Europe, and though he rode in a sitting rather than straight-legged position, he certainly did not use the short stirrup leathers assumed by some historians; a Middle Eastern cavalryman rode with stirrups that would touch his ankle bone when his legs hung loose. Horses seem to have been trained to avoid

Kitab al Baytarah, *'Book of Veterinary Information'*. A man wearing the fur-lined hat of the military elite trains a war-horse. (Topkapi Library, Ms. Ahmet III 2115, Istanbul, Turkey)

spear thrusts, and a horse-archer's mount was trained to continue in a straight line, ignoring pressure from the rider's knees until it felt a pull on the reins.

Unlike the knightly elite of Europe, the professional Muslim cavalryman was expected to arm himself without the help of a servant. Training also included the use and maintenance of military equipment, where to keep it in camp so that it could be found in the dark, how to put on armour at night and how to take it off even while his horse was in motion. The Fatimid army of Egypt was greatly concerned with correct positioning in the ranks, discipline and the ability of cavalry squadrons to manoeuvre in unison. In later *furusiya* manuals, several manoeuvres look more like square-bashing than realistic fighting exercises. They were probably designed to strengthen team work, and to improve unit cohesion while riding at different speeds and wheeling in various directions.

The Bow

Few unit exercises involved the bow; training in its use was largely an individual matter. The Middle Eastern tradition of horse-archery was based upon 'shower-shooting' in volleys, often while stationary. This tactic was more versatile than Central Asian horse-archery and needed less logistical backup. In the 10th century archers trained by shooting at a stuffed straw animal in a four-wheeled cart that was rolled downhill or pulled by a horseman. A fully competent 13th century archer could shoot five arrows, held in the left hand with the bow, in two and a half seconds. Another five arrows were then snatched from a quiver.

Most archery training emphasised dexterity rather than accuracy. Nevertheless, a skilled archer was expected to hit a metre-wide target at 75 metres. (Closer-range archery training had a 6½-metre training distance.) Training concentrated on three disciplines: shooting level, upwards or downwards, the latter two generally from horseback while moving. A horse-archer would probably have been able to loose five arrows at between 30 and five metres from an enemy when charging at full speed. He dropped his reins as he shot, but might use a strap from the reins to the ring-finger of his right hand to enable him to regain them quickly. The

Lustre-ware plate, 12th century Egypt. A Fatimid nobleman or officer wears a massive turban indicating his status. (Museum of Islamic Art, inv. 13477, Cairo, Egypt)

section on archery in al Tarsusi, the famous military author of the late 12th century who wrote for Saladin, offers the following advice to Muslim archers fighting the Crusaders:

When shooting at a horseman who is armoured or otherwise untouchable, shoot at his horse to dismount him. When shooting at a horseman who is not moving, aim at the saddle-bow and thus hit the man if [the arrow flies] too high and the horse if too low. If his back is turned, aim at the spot between his shoulders. If he charges with a sword shoot at him, but not from too far off for if you miss he might hit you with his sword. Never shoot blindly!

This advice was based in Fatimid traditions. The manual stated that if a horse-archer had a sword, he should dangle it from his right wrist by its hilt-loop while shooting. If he had a lance, he should put it under his right thigh unless he also had a sword, in which case the lance went beneath the left thigh. A group of horse-archers was advised to disperse around a bunched-up enemy but should reassemble if the foe came close. If encountered on a road, the enemy should be kept on the archer's

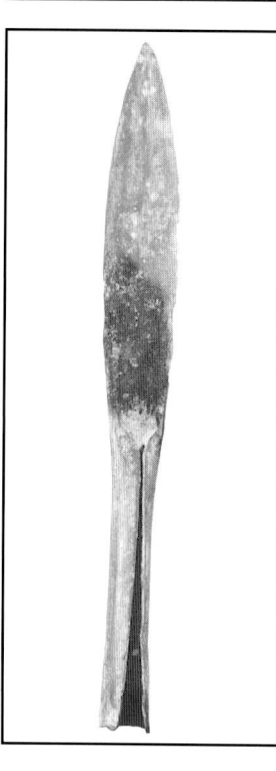

Left: Bronze spearhead, said to be Ayyubid late 12th/early 13th century. (Islamic Mus., Mazar, Jordan)

Right: Cast-iron sword guard from al Rabadhah in Arabia, 8th/9th century. (King Sa'ud Univ., Riyadh, Saudi Arabia)

Below: Second sword of Caliph Musta'sim, mid-13th century Iraq. The pommel and studs on the hilt are later Ottoman Turkish additions. (Topkapi Armoury, Istanbul, Turkey)

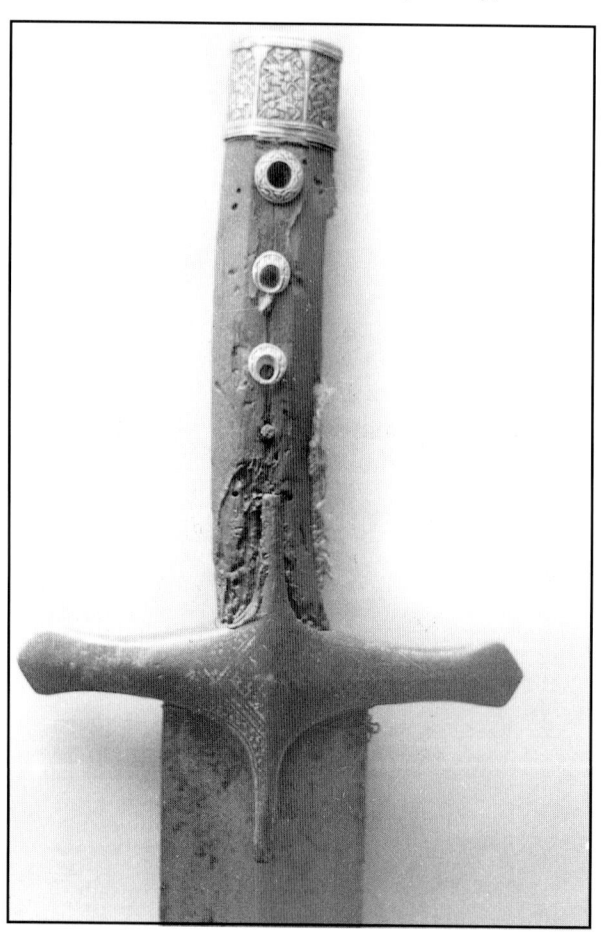

Sword of an unnamed Abbasid Caliph, 13th/14th century Iraq or Egypt. (Topkapi Armoury, Istanbul, Turkey)

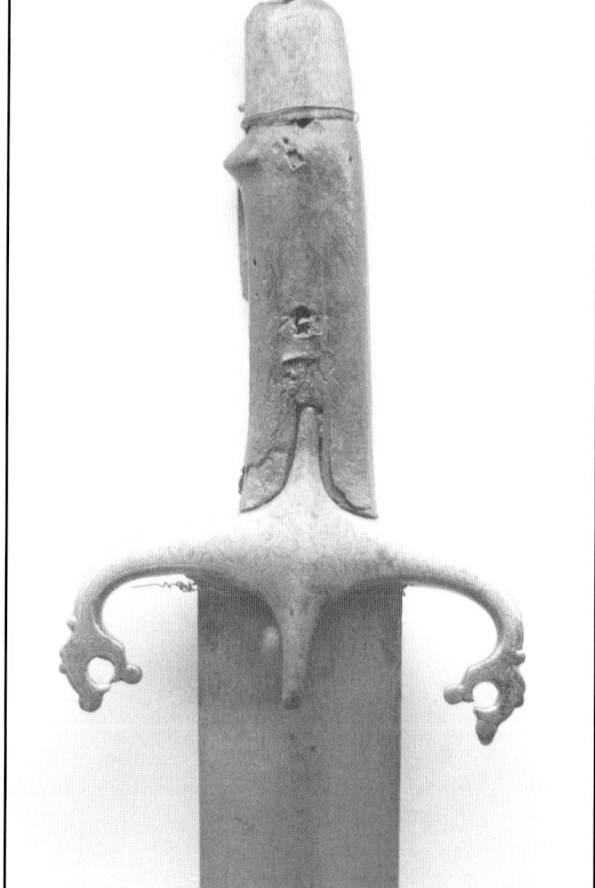

left, but if this was impossible, the men should stay in line with their shields raised.

Shooting involved a sequence of skills: *itar* or stringing the bow; *qabda* or grasping the bow in the left hand; *tafwiq* or nocking an arrow in the string; *aqd* or locking the string in the right hand; *madd* or drawing back to the eye-brow, ear-lobe, moustache, chin or breastbone; *nazar* or aiming with any necessary corrections; and *itlaq* or loosing the arrow. Shooting was done in three ways: 'snatched' with the draw and release in one continuous movement; 'held' with a slow draw and a short pause before releasing; and 'twisted' with a partial draw followed by a pause then a snatched final draw and release. Men were advised to vary their techniques according to the tactical situation and to avoid tiring themselves.

Professional archers were trained to shoot from horseback, or standing, sitting, squatting and kneeling. They learned to shoot over fortifications and from beneath shields. There were several strengths of bow for different purposes, and they are distinguished by their draw-weights. A standard war weapon was from 50 kg up to a maximum of 75 kg. Three types of draw were used: the weak Mediterranean or European draw; the three-fingered *daniyyat* or Persian draw; and the powerful *bazm* or Turkish thumb-draw. A protective leather flap inside the fingers could be used with the Persian draw, and a protective thumb-ring with the Turkish thumb-draw.

The Spear

A professional *faris* was trained to use his spear in a greater variety of ways than his European counterpart. In the long-established two-handed style, a rider slacked his reins as he lowered his lance-point, then dropped them as he struck the enemy. Such a thrust could pierce two layers of mail and come out the other side. Even so, Usama recommended the couched lance technique used by his Crusader foes, a style subsequently known as 'The Syrian Attack'. Later in the 12th century al Tarsusi advised cavalry to attack infantry with both spear and sword.

Other descriptions of cavalry combat mention the use of shields to parry rather than simply to obstruct a foe's lance blow. Among various spear exercises was the *birjas* game, where a charging horseman was expected to remove the topmost of a column of wooden blocks without knocking down any other blocks.

The Sword

Sword fencing was also highly developed. Several detailed accounts of close combat from the 10th and 12th centuries illustrate the terrifying impact of a sword as well as the precision with which a fully trained *faris* could deliver a blow. On one occasion a Persian cavalryman charged into the midst of an Arab ruler's bodyguard and injured the enemy commander with carefully aimed cuts at his head,

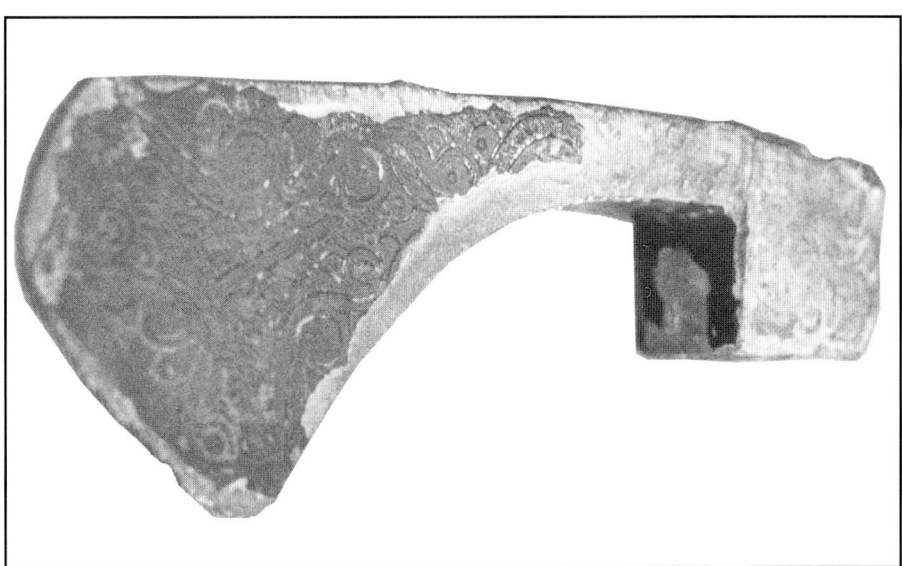

Silver-covered iron war axe, 12th/13th century Syria (Victoria and Albert Mus., Inv. M.145-1919, London, England)

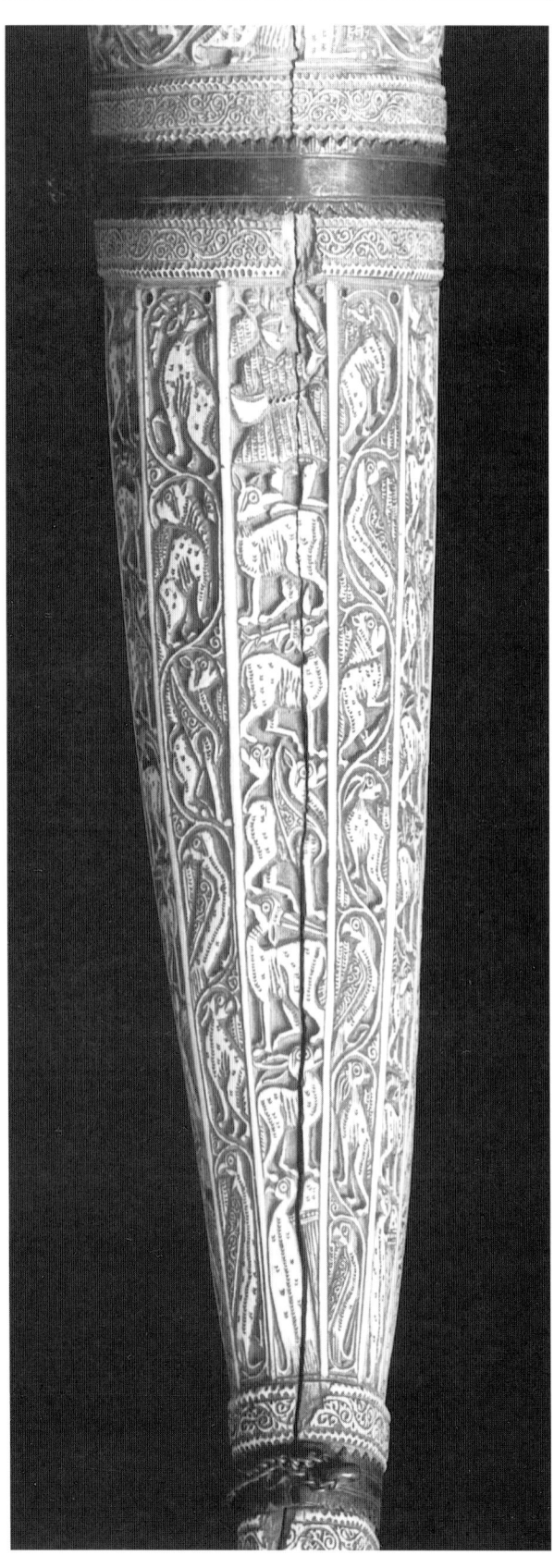

shoulder and elbow. An Arab cavalryman then struck at him, first severing the Persian's index finger – which suggests that this was over the quillons of his sword – then his middle finger. When the Persian dropped his sword the Arab promptly cut off his head. Sword exercises in *furusiya* manuals emphasised the strength and accuracy of cutting, but not thrusting. In one 'game' men on horseback rode past a line of green reeds, slicing sections off each reed in successive passes. As a result, the power of a good sword-cut could be devastating. To quote Usama:

'I had a fight with an Isma'ili [Assassin] who had a dagger in his hand while I had my sword. He rushed at me with the dagger and I hit him in the middle of his forearm as he was grasping the hilt of the dagger and holding the blade close to his forearm. My blow cut about four inches off the dagger-blade and severed his forearm in two. The mark of the edge of the dagger was left on the edge of my sword. A craftsman in our town, on seeing it, said: "I can remove this dent." But I said: "Leave it as it is. It is the best thing on my sword." The mark is there to this day.'

Other cavalry training involved the use of cover and dead ground and the crossing of rivers. (The ability to swim was considered second in importance only to literacy.)

HOME AND BARRACKS

Medieval Islamic civilisation, particularly among military groups, had great respect for individual worth and personal achievement. Attitudes were in many ways closer to those of the modern world than to those of medieval Europe. Overcoming natural cowardice, for example, was regarded as

Carved ivory horn or 'oliphant' from southern Italy. It is in Fatimid style and was either made locally by Muslim craftsmen from Sicily or was imported from Egypt. Note the turbaned, mail-clad warrior near the top, armed with a sword and shield. Such huge and magnificent horns would have been prized possessions among the military elite. (Musée Crozatier, Le Puy, France)

more admirable than feeling no fear. (Feeling no fear was often attributed to stupidity.) Military service was also considered to involve an element of personal humiliation through submission to orders, but at the same time, the military elite were also something of a social elite. As one Arab replied when taunted for his humble origins: *'My family line begins with me, yours ends with you!'*

Protection of the weak by the strong was a powerful ideal and romantic ideals of honour, particularly among the Arabs, were remarkably similar to those of Western European chivalry. For example a cavalryman who felt that his honour had been tarnished by being struck by a second-rate soldier would charge among the enemy's ranks just so that he could return the blow. The beliefs and attitudes of the Turkish warrior classes were different; the Turks believed that they were destined to rule the world. Even after becoming Muslim, they continued to see themselves as a chosen people who had saved Islam in its hour of crisis.

The differing attitudes of Turkish, Persian and Arab soldiers was also reflected in their literary tastes. Tales of love and war written for the Turks had much in common with French *Chansons de Geste*, whereas Persian stories tended to focus on a lost imperial past, a clash of titanic heroes and the splendour of courtly life. The Arabic epic tradition, which reached its final form during the Crusades, showed deeper interest in human relations, the emotions of battle and the tense relationship between men and women, with the leading character often being female. There were also elements of sex and violence: an enemy warrior-heroine with a 'bottom like a narcissus flower' final succumbs to the hero, and, of course, falls in love with him.

Music played a very important part in the culture of Arab, Persian and Turkish military elites, but was regarded with deep suspicion by the religious leadership. Chess was associated with older and wiser warriors, and youngsters preferred faster, gambling games. The Saracen soldier's love of perfumes and flowers was seen as effeminate by the rougher Crusaders, but scents cooled a man in the heat of the Middle East, while flowers and fragrant leaves flavoured his drinks. Of course the Muslim warrior drank more than mere 'sherbet' –

Chess was regarded as the game of the ruling and officer classes. It had been introduced from India in the early Middle Ages and was then passed on to Europe. Most chess pieces were abstract in shape, in deference to Muslim disapproval of three-dimensional images, but several surviving ivory chess 'knights' are small mounted warriors, normally armed with sword and shield. This example comes from Iran and probably dates from the 12th century. (Met. Mus. of Art, New York, USA

alcoholic beverages were widespread. A thick sweet slightly fermented juice made from dried grapes or dates was acceptable, and the Turks also drank a form of beer called *buzah*.

More is known about the social attitudes of the officer class than of ordinary soldiers. The Muslim elite was very concerned with etiquette: the correct way of eating; respect for age and women; and 'moderation in all things'. But where romance was concerned, they showed less restraint; pursuit of the fair sex was considered normal for a young man, though quite separate from the question of marriage. As Kai Ka'us, ruler of Gurgan, wrote for his son in AD1082: *'Marry a woman of honourable family, because men marry in order to have a lady for the house and not to indulge in sexual pleasure. To satisfy your desires you can buy slave-girls in the bazaar, which involves less expense and less trouble.'*

The idea that the Muslim warrior's ideal woman was fat is also untrue. A beauty was described as slender like a cane or twig, with a pale face, long dark hair, large dark eyes, a straight nose, a small mouth, bright red lips, a small bosom, waist, hands and feet but wide hips. She was also highly sexed.

The significance of *jihad* and religious motivation may have become exaggerated but they were important. *Jihad* itself was never supposed to force conversion to Islam; it was intended to increase the power of Islam and to defend Muslims. The Crusader conquest of parts of Syria and the Holy Land was, in fact, received with apathy outside the areas immediately concerned. Yet the savagery of the newly arrived 'Franks' (Western European Christians) was noted, and some scholars who understood Crusader motivation worked for a revival of the *jihad* spirit. Once it did re-emerge, it was a Sunni or 'orthodox' Muslim phenomenon aimed as much against 'heretical' Shi'a Muslims as against the Crusaders. However, how much influence scholarly works on *jihad* had on ordinary soldiers remains unknown.

As far as the professional soldier was concerned the rules of war, or *siyar*, had been established back in the 8th century. They were rooted in religion, and any educated soldier knew them well. Basically they consisted of the rules of *jihad* (who could and could not be fought and under what circumstances), *'aman* (when and where safe-conduct should be offered to an enemy) and *hudnah* (the rules regulating truces). Sometimes such regulations were highly specific, dealing with the preservation of fruit trees and beehives. Among the most important practical regulations were those dealing with obedience to orders, keeping one's word – even to an enemy, not harming women, children, old men, non-military slaves or religious figures (unless the latter were spies), and causing no more devastation than was militarily necessary. Male prisoners could be killed or enslaved, though only for good reason, whereas female prisoners should be provided with transport into captivity. Clearly Muslim soldiers and their commanders did not always live up to such high standards, but at least the *siyar* was there as an ideal – which is more than can be said for European warfare against non-Christians.

The Muslim soldier was also rather superstitious. Small totemic swords, magic daggers and written charms have been found in many areas, though very little is now known about how they were supposed to work. Astrology, the interpretation of dreams, and predictions were widespread

The back of a gold-inlaid polished steel mirror from early 13th century Turkish Anatolia (modern Turkey), decorated with a horseman with a hunting hawk on his wrist. (Topkapi Mus., Istanbul, Turkey)

and may have been particularly characteristic of the military – whose lives and careers were even more uncertain than those of ordinary men.

For several centuries the military elites of the Muslim Middle East had been firmly based in cities and towns. Even the Saljuq Turks soon settled into urban citadels and became, like their Arab and Persian predecessors, patrons of culture and religion. The core elites of their armies also lived within cities, though for several generations Turcoman tribal troops tended to live in tents beyond the walls.

In Fatimid Egypt the Caliph's guard regiments had their *hujra* barracks within the palace grounds. Other regiments were sited elsewhere in the city, though none has yet been identified by archaeologists. The palatial houses of senior Fatimid officers were also defended by personal guards. Evidence from cities like Mosul in northern Iraq suggests that the tents of a large garrison could eventually have been replaced by houses, thus creating a new suburb with its own special markets and other facilities. At the same time, even professional troops would gradually have acquired parallel civilian jobs.

Little is known of life within the *hujra* or barracks, but information from 10th century Tarsus shows that some included their own armouries and workshops or even had shops underneath them and used the rents from these to support the volunteer soldiers who lived above. By the 14th/15th century the barracks of Egyptian *mamluks* had even developed as centres of literary endeavour, poetry and such, alongside the military training. In 11th century Baghdad the most powerful officers lived in palaces overlooking the river, while over the road were barracks and mosques for their troops, and stables for cavalry horses.

Blocks of apartments and perhaps barracks which characterised great cities like Cairo had much in common with the towering tenements of ancient Rome. But most soldiers may have lived in private houses. This would be in keeping with the concern for privacy which lies at the heart of the Muslim way of life. Many ordinary city houses have been excavated by archaeologists, and, like Roman houses, they faced inwards, built around a courtyard. An extended family unit including several generations usually lived in one house and maintained close links with brothers, sisters, cousins, and clan or tribal members near and far. The *harim* or 'sacred area' was the women's domain, and the husband had his own room at its edge. The men of the house also needed a guest area for entertaining male visitors. (Women entertaining lady visitors within the *harim*.) Family life was very close-knit, with business, education, entertainment and even amorous adventures taking place within a closed but extended family. The head of such a family might,

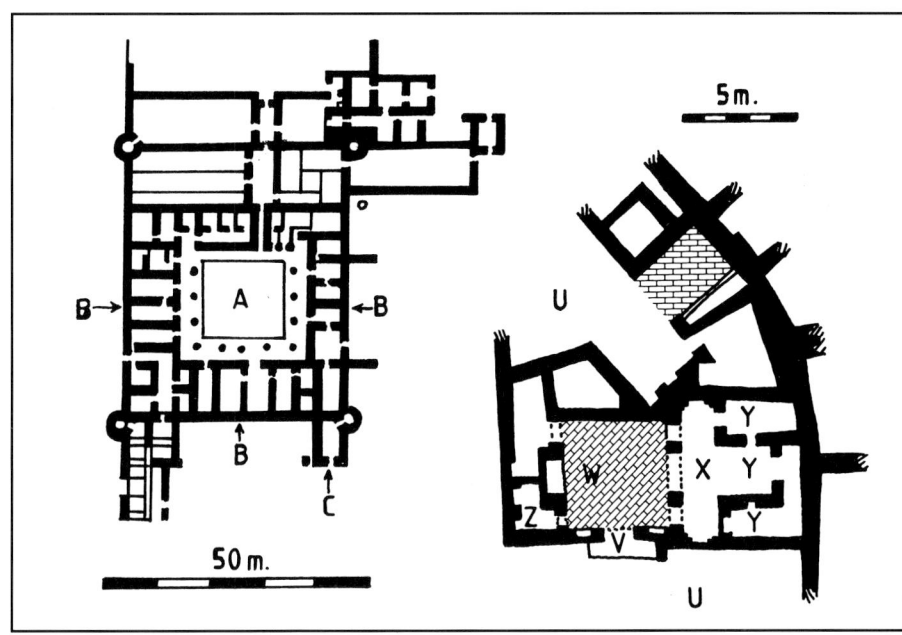

Left: Plan of the large house of a rich family near Khatlon, Tajikstan, 9th–11th century (A: courtyard; B: three separate series of living quarters; C: bathhouse).

Right: Plan of an ordinary multi-storey city house in Fustat, Cairo, 11th–12th century (U – streets; V – entrance; W – paved courtyard; X – portico of house; Y – bayt system of downstairs rooms; Z – latrine).

like Usama Ibn Muqidh in AD1154, find himself responsible for 50 people: men, women, his own and his brother's children, and various servants.

Marriage was a duty for a Muslim; not doing so for any reason other than health was sinful. The choice of a partner was generally left to the mother, a female relation or a professional female betrother. Cousins were seen as ideal spouses because their character would be well known, and such a marriage further strengthened family bonds. A man was permitted four wives, but it was considered better to have just one. The law insisted that each be treated exactly equally, even in the most private matters. Divorce was easier and certainly more acceptable than in Christian society and may have served as a counterbalance to an individual's initial lack of choice. Yet at the same time, Usama was shocked by the Crusaders' lack of sexual jealousy and by their lack of personal modesty.

Far from being isolated, Muslim women had access to public life – though the public world had no access to them. On at least two occasions the women of Usama's family seized weapons when Shayzar was attacked, and an 11th century reference to a lady wielding great political influence 'because she won over the soldiers' wives' suggests that a soldier may have been something less than the master within his own house.

The bonds which kept the military classes together were quite distinct from family ties. *Asabiyah* tribal solidarity was still strong, and played a very important role throughout the 12th century. It could link up with *istina'*, the sense of obligation between soldiers and a 'patron' or commander who was seen as their foster father. In the 10th century the swearing of public mutual oaths of loyalty had been an important way of cementing the relationship between rulers, officers

Top row: Two views of 13th century Iraqi houses from the Maqamat *of al Hariri, painted by al Wasiti in AD1237 (Bib. Nat., Paris, Ms. Ar. 5847). On the left two men approach a rich man's house while three servants sit on a brick bench outside. On the right a drinking party takes place inside a house.*

Bottom row: Three views of Egyptian or Syrian town houses on a 14th/15th century Mamluk silver and gold inlaid brass bowl. (Bargello Museum, Florence)

and men, but these were less important during the Crusader era. Gifts of clothes, arms, armour and horse harness enabled a leader to reward his followers, since status was shown by the richness of a man's dress and weaponry.

Medieval Middle Eastern costume was functional rather than formal; role, sex, religion and ethnic origin were indicated by the quality and colour of cloth and minor variations in the cut of clothes. The variety of dyes, patterns and fabrics was much wider than in medieval Europe, and elite troops wore magnificently distinctive dress, though not real uniforms. Professional Middle Eastern soldiers, though not North Africans, tended to wear Persian and Turkish rather than Arab costume when on duty. The most obvious items of dress were a double-breasted coat, a *hiyasa* belt incorporating decorative metal plates, and the *sharbush* stiff fur-edged cap with a triangular plate at the front. This could be replaced by a *qalawta* cap. In Saljuq Persia another elaborate cap for high ranking military figures was the *dushakh*, which had a double-pointed shape.

Military jewellery ranged from the magnificent *hafir* or turban decoration of a ruler to the *siwarayn* or bracelets allowed senior officers and the *tawq* or

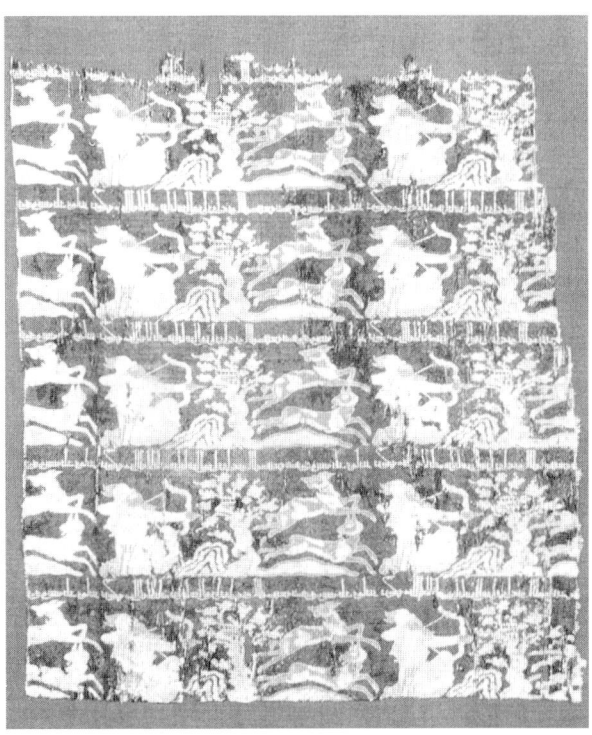

Above: 12th–13th century ewer from Iran. Inlaid metalwork would have been among the most prized possessions of a successful soldier. They have little value as bullion, being made of bronze with a tiny amount of gold or silver inlay, and would not have appealed to the average looting Crusader. But their exquisite craftsmanship made them valuable in the eyes of the educated Muslim elite. (British Museum, London, England)

Right: Woven silk cloth from Iran, 9th–12th century. Not surprisingly Western European Crusaders were amazed by the apparent wealth of the Muslim world when they found people wearing fabric like this. In reality it was the technological sophistication of Middle Eastern weavers which made such patterns possible. (Mus. of Art, Cleveland, Ohio, USA)

Embroidered silk tombcover from Iran, late 10th century. This is an example of the richest fabrics produced in the Islamic countries at the time. (Mus. of Art, Cleveland, Ohio, USA)

Right: Fragment of imported Indian resist-dyed (batik) cotton cloth from Qusayr in Egypt, probably from the 11th century. This light and relatively inexpensive fabric could have been worn by any but the poorest people of the Middle East. (Location unknown)

Printed cotton fabric from Fatimid Egypt, 10th–12th century. The technique of printing such large areas did not reach Europe for several centuries. (Mus. of Art, Cleveland, Ohio, USA)

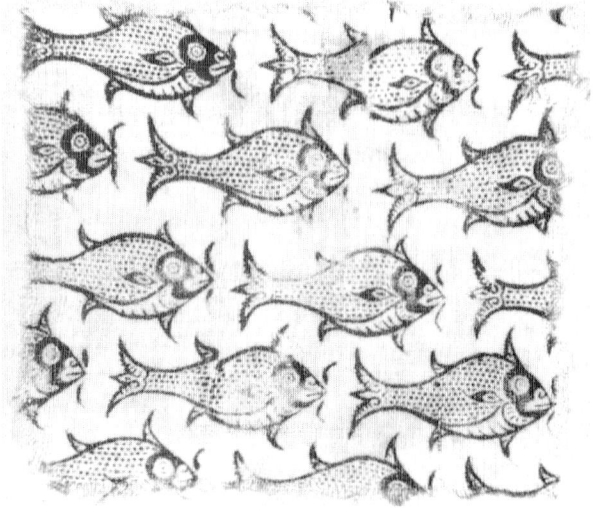

necklace given to a successful commander. Ordinary officers wore what they could afford, and this, along with the fact that Muslim armies were normally paid in cash, explains the Crusaders' enthusiasm for stripping their dead foes.

Most cavalryman had only one war-horse, and a great deal of effort went into keeping it in peak condition. Mounts were normally tethered in an open air *mizalla* or paddock with a shaded shelter of palm leaves, but a surprise enemy attack could find the horses dispersed to pasture, as happened to Nur al Din in 1163. However, even a small castle like Shayzar had its *istabl* or stables for war-horses and pack animals. The animals were hobbled by three legs, rather than four as in Europe, and got their

feed in nose-bags rather than mangers on the wall. Qualified staff, listed as military servants, looked after horse and harness, a *ghulam* or stable-boy kept the place clean, a *sa'is* or groom looked after one or more animals and a *shaddad* or harnessman took care of the tack. A large stable might also have its own resident *baytar* or vet.

MILITARY CAREERS

Known examples of military careers inevitably reflect the successful or literate elite, but in highly literate armies like those of the medieval Muslim Middle East, quite a lot of information survives about 'middle ranking' soldiers.

The most detailed record of a 12th century military career is that of Usama Ibn Munqidh, who was born into the long-established Arab warrior family which ruled Shayzar castle. At the age of 13 he saw his first Crusader assault on Shayzar. At 14 he began studying grammar, and at 21 he met a 'Frank' or Western European for the first time. Usama trained as a soldier, and witnessed a further four attacks on Shayzar, until at 24, the year his grammar tutor left, he took part in his first small battle against a Crusader force. At 31 his first surviving male child was born. At 35 Usama left Shayzar after quarrelling with the head of his family, and within a short time he enrolled in Nur al Din's army. Between the ages of 35 and 43 he took part in many campaigns against Crusaders, Armenians and fellow Muslims. Then he took service with the ruler of Damascus. At 49 Usama was entrusted with a diplomatic mission to Fatimid Egypt, after which he joined the Egyptian army and spent the next ten years fighting Crusaders in southern Palestine, going on diplomatic missions and getting caught up in the murderous politics of the declining Fatimid Caliphate. He then returned to Nur al Din whom he served for a further ten years, and eventually retired to the cultured Artuqid Turkish court of the Diyarbakir region where he concentrated on writing poetry, books of good advice and his famous *Memoires*. At 79 Usama Ibn Munqidh was summoned back to Damascus by Saladin and became a respected teacher, supported by an *iqta* 'fief' or estate near the town of Ma'arat al Nu'man. Usama died at the age of 93 – an astonishing age for the 12th century – and he was buried on the mountain overlooking Damascus.

On retirement a senior officer might be rewarded with the command of a town's police force or militia. Some were given low administrative ranks or simply retired to a frontier *ribat* for military volunteers. An injured or retired officer would normally lose his *iqta*, but this could be replaced by a money allowance. The little information that survives about ordinary soldiers suggests that many retired as merchants, shopkeepers or owners of mule trains, while others became pillars of the religious establishment – even if only as local hermits. A certain Jawad, an expert swordsman in Shayzar, was met by Usama many years later: '*I saw him in Damascus. He had become a dealer in fodder and was selling barley and hay. He was old and looked like a worn-out water-bag, too weak even to keep the mice away from his fodder – much less keep away people.'* The aged Usama wrote a poem on his own condition late in life:

*But now I have become like an idle girl who lies
On stuffed cushions behind screens and curtains.
  I have almost become rotten from lying still so long,
Just as the sword of Indian steel becomes rusty when left long in its sheath.
  After being dressed in coats of mail, I now dress in robes of fine fabric.
  Woe to me and to the fabrics!*

On Duty

The order of rank in 11th–13th century Muslim armies varied and was flexible; individuals rose by merit and by luck from humble origins to the top echelons. One example was the 11th century governor Anushtakin al Dizbari. He was a Turkish slave from Khuttal in Central Asia who took his name from his first owner, a Fatimid officer called Dizbar. After training in administrative and military duties, Anushtakin al Dizbari joined the Fatimid army, served in Syria and rose to become governor of Palestine around the age of 35.

Pay reflected rank, the status of the unit and the wealth of the ruler it served. Even so, soldiers generally earned more than skilled craftsmen – increasingly so up to the 13th century. In the Fatimid army, provincial garrison troops were paid directly by the Treasury in cash, as were soldiers listed according to their *hujra* barracks. Professional mercenaries were paid individually in cash by the government, while others received their pay via their officers. Such payments to the *jaysh* or army could have been every two, three or four months.

Early 13th century minai-ware bowl from Rayy in Iran. The man on the right carries a polo-stick in addition to his weapons. (Brooklyn Museum, inv. 86.227.60, New York, USA)

Right: 12th/13th century lustre-ware plate from Iran. The potters of the Middle East learned much from China and then added their own techniques. Lustre-glazing gave pottery an almost metallic appearance. (Ashmolean Mus., Oxford, England)

They generally seem to have been made at a special parade, and it is interesting to note that the Saljuq *Siyasat Nama* or 'book of government' strongly recommended a ruler to be present when his troops got their money so that he got the credit.

Smaller armies of the Fertile Crescent which emerged from the fragmentation of the Great Saljuq Empire were paid in a similar way. Regular soldiers in early 12th century Damascus got a monthly *jamakiyah* or wage, and senior men were supported by *iqta* fiefs as far afield as central Syria, central Lebanon and what is now southern Jordan. Nur al Din's *askar* were not only paid but also equipped by him, though their weapons were kept in a government *zardkhanah* or arsenal to be distributed at the start of a campaign.

Payment in Saladin's army was similar to that of the preceding Fatimids and pay differentials between ranks could be immense. Junior recruits received little, but the biggest salary increases were from ordinary soldier to junior officer, and from high officer to men holding senior command. Professional cavalrymen also had a regular food allowance, usually as grain to feed their horses, and an additional payment was given at the start of a campaign, supposedly to cover additional active service costs.

A cavalryman's greatest expense was his warhorse, along with several cheaper baggage animals.

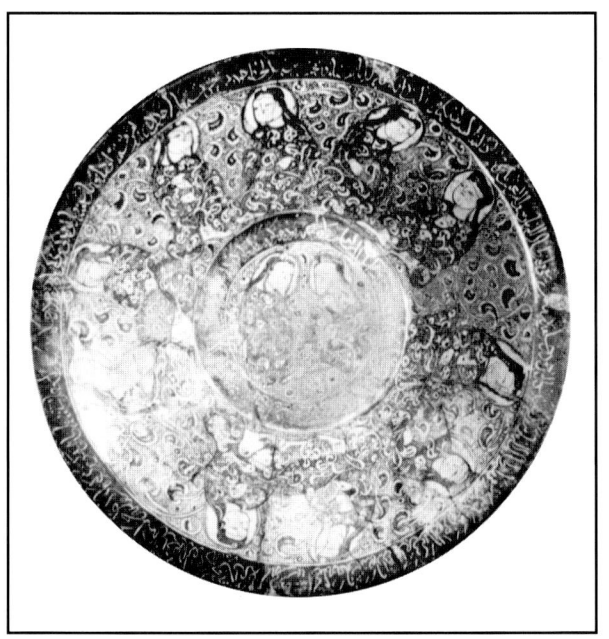

The huge variations in price reflected the quality of animal: an ordinary horse in 12th century Egypt was worth about three camels, a really fine-bred stallion 200 camels. A decorated harness could also prove expensive for officers. Although a soldier often received weapons free from the arsenal, their cost could be deducted from his pay if they were lost. There is some evidence to suggest that troops also purchased their own equipment; this could range from a simple lamellar cuirass worth 'two sheep in autumn' to a senior officer's decorated military belt costing more than an ordinary soldier's annual pay.

Rulers might wear mail under their ordinary clothes as a precaution against assassination, but normal armour hung very heavy on a man's shoulders and would only be put on just before going into action. The sequence for putting on cavalry equipment was basically the same as in Western Europe: first came a shirt or padded garment; then a mail hauberk and a cuirass, if worn; next came the sword-belt, a separate archery belt, a mace in its holder; then the shield and spear. Many Turkish warriors also seem to have hung amulets against the 'evil eye' from their body or weaponry. It was common to put a small dagger inside one's riding boot, and detailed evidence from two centuries later added a wooden spoon, a small leather bag for salt, a kerchief, a sharpening stone, eating knives, a comb in a case, a leather cup and a waterproof felt cape to the fully equipped cavalryman's kit.

Battles were infrequent, and the average Muslim cavalryman spent most of his time on other duties. A *tawashi* cavalryman in Nur al Din's army was expected to do a certain number of months active service each year, though quite where is not known. While elite units would normally remain close to a ruler, this was not invariably the case. The *halqa* of Saladin's army was almost always near the sultan, and the elite *jandariya* formed an Ayyubid ruler's guard in peace and in war. They also served as the sultan's messengers, inflicted punishments, guarded arsenals and arms depots. *Jandariya* units could also garrison vital places in time of danger. *Tawashis* first appeared as eunuchs in charge of military training, but by the 12th century they were an important cavalry force,

The stables of Azraq castle in Jordan, built in AD 1236/7. (author's photograph)

usually stationed at the centre of an army and apparently never used as garrison troops. Under Saladin many *tawashi* elite horsemen appear to have been slave-recruited *mamluks*, while his *qaraghulam* or 'black *ghulam*' cavalry were of inferior status. The use of the term *qara* or black probably stems from the Turkish symbolic use of this word to denote low-born people of obscure origin as opposed to *aq* or white people of aristocratic birth – not black Africans.

Military reviews were central to a Middle Eastern soldier's duties. Men were drawn up for inspection in squadrons, 'alert and brave' and wearing their best if the ruler was to appear. In Fatimid Egypt the men often got special parade equipment from arsenals and treasuries, but observers also noted several cases of confusion, when troops did not know what to do or where to go, and they were sometimes given *madarij* papers explaining their precise position on parade. Reviews enabled troops to be assessed; the best were allocated to the ruler's own regiments, the average were sent off to garrison other cities, and the worst were used as provincial police.

More time was spent in tedious guard duties. In 11th century Egypt the night garrison of the Caliph's palace complex consisted of 500 cavalry and 500 infantry. Elsewhere the garrison of a 12th or 13th century city was responsible for guarding the wall, gates, citadel, parade ground and government offices. A strategic city like Mosul contained 1,500 cavalry and infantry in AD1108/9, but other smaller towns to the north-west were garrisoned by just ten horsemen and an unknown number of foot soldiers. Garrisons also escorted merchant caravans between cities in areas infested with bandits.

ON CAMPAIGN

Campaigns normally started in spring or autumn; late autumn and winter were unpopular as this was when auxiliary troops went home to plant winter crops. Winters could also be bleak and wet in Syria and northern Mesopotamia. Summer was often impractical because of the heat and dust, particularly in Iraq, and finding adequate drinking water for large numbers of troops could also be a problem in late summer. Many important operations were carried out by just a few hundred men, but in larger armies troops would be divided into tactical units, the smallest of which would have between 70 and 100 soldiers. On active service cavalry units of around 500 men were formed to mount an ambush, undertake reconnaissance ahead of the main army, form advance or rearguards or a banner-guard, protect the supply train or raid that of the enemy (see MAA 171 *Saladin and the Saracens*, and Campaign 19 *Hattin 1187*).

Marching was accompanied by military music

from trumpets and drums carried on mules, and was used particularly in enemy territory to maintain morale. The later European tradition of military music clearly owed a great deal to that of the Ottoman Turks and their predecessors. A small army could cover 30 kilometres a day, which suggests that any infantry would also have been mounted. A large army with a complete baggage train would not have covered such a distance since the train itself could include 7,000 merchants – from farriers for the horses to bath-owners for their riders, not to mention a field hospital.

Army doctors were expected to have an almost modern 'bedside manner' so as to reassure their patients; as Kai Ka'us advised his son in AD1082:

'His person and dress must always be clean and he should wear pleasant perfume. When visiting a patient he must always look cheerful and untroubled, with pleasant words to encourage the sick. A doctor's heartening words to his patient increase the natural heat of his temperament [i.e. strengthen his powers of recovery].'

Merchants of the *suq al 'askar* or 'army market' supplied food which soldiers bought with their wages. Little is known about what the men actually ate, though an interesting reference from 13th century Turkish Anatolia mentions a soldier keeping an orange in his bowcase as a snack. Otherwise soldiers probably ate the same simple diet as other people, largely consisting of what is now called pitta bread, as well as assorted beans, dates, fruit, milk products, chicken and mutton. Vegetables were an essential and healthy part of every meal, for as the Arab proverb said: *'A table without vegetables is like an old man without wisdom.'* Surviving medieval cookery books naturally reflect the tastes of the ruling elite rather than an army on campaign, but medieval Islamic cuisine was generally much simpler than the elaborate concoctions enjoyed by the European ruling classes. The following instructions for a simple egg dish come from a 13th century Iraqi cookbook and could well have been a dish made in camp:

Put some sesame oil in a frying pan. Celery leaves

Among figures around the outer edge of this early 13th century 'battle plate' from Iran are a retainer with a bow-case on his hip and a ruler carrying the animal-headed form of mace reserved for leading figures. (Freer Gallery of Art, inv. 43.3, Washington, USA)

taken from their stalks are then chopped, added to the oil and fried. Then sprinkle over this sufficient amounts of cinnamon, mastic, coriander, and caraway. Next pour some vinegar into the mixture, as much as required, colouring with a little saffron. When the mixture has been heated, add a little salt then break the egg and add to it. Cover the pan until the egg is cooked and serve. (D. Waines, *In a Caliph's Kitchen*, London 1989)

The most vulnerable moment was considered to be the *nuzul* or 'halting' when an extended marching army congregated to set up camp. This was when elite cavalry units, however weary, had to watch for a sudden enemy attack. The camp itself consisted of concentric circles of tents round that of the leader, with guard-posts and a ditch around the perimeter. An elite cavalry unit would also be stationed up to a mile away in the direction of the enemy. The men were advised not to make fires as this attracted trouble, but if they were really cold they could dig a hole and light a hidden fire at the bottom.

Battle and the Aftermath

Such caution inevitably influenced the conduct of ordinary soldiers. Most leaders realised that battles were won or lost in the minds of the combatants. Saladin, despite several defeats at the hands of the Third Crusade, never allowed his army to be destroyed, and eventually wore down his enemies so that the Crusade simply stalled. Even at the level of the common soldier, training emphasised checking thickets and hollows for potential ambushes while pursuing an apparently defeated foe. This was in stark contrast to the 'gung ho' behaviour of Crusader forces.

In a full-scale battle, an identifying battle-cry was agreed before combat. The commander made his morale boosting speech, usually of a religious nature, banners, probably associated with earlier Muslim heroes or Caliphs, were waved and men were ordered to stay close to their weapons until the fighting began. In general, Muslim officers showed

Maqamat *of al Hariri illustrated by al Wasiti, Baghdad* AD1237, *showing the Caliph's army on the march. (Bibliotheque Nationale, Ms. Ar. 5847, f.94, Paris, France)*

The 'Freer Canteen', a large silver-inlaid bronze flask from the early 13th century Jazira region, showing horse-armour. (Freer Gallery of Art, no. 41.10, Washington, USA)

great concern for the safety of their followers, as Usama again made clear during his first battle against a band of Crusaders:

'They [the Crusaders] had been reinforced that night by sixty horsemen and sixty infantry. They drove us out of the valley and we retreated ... Seeing us the Franks shouted aloud. Death seemed an easy thing to me in comparison with losing all those people under my command, so I turned back against one of their leading horsemen ... and thrust my lance into his chest.'

Theoretical works written for Saladin also emphasised the need to put only the best men in charge of assault troops or other important units. Military leaders were also warned not to neglect the interests of labourers and other non-combatants. The soldiers themselves were also reluctant to shed too much Muslim blood if they were fighting men of their own faith. Apart from religious considerations, late 11th/early 12th century soldiers did not know who their future employer or ally might be and so wanted to avoid blood-feuds between families. On the other hand professional troops could fight even if their position was hopeless – just long enough to demonstrate their own military value before surrendering in the hope of being re-enlisted by the victor. On the other side, a commander should, according to al Harawi, *'attempt to win over the hearts of [enemy] citizens, soldiers, officers and leaders by all possible means. He should communicate with them and offer the commanders and nobility whatever they want.'*

Tactics were the concern of the commander rather than the ordinary cavalryman. Although the Fatimid army relied primarily on infantry, in battle its heavy cavalry would be stationed behind the infantry, and light cavalry on the wings. Each cavalry squadron stood ready to charge through gaps in the infantry line which would open up, presumably when a signal was made. The horsemen would then try to strike the enemy in his flank. The cavalry in line formation, making limited attacks and withdrawals, with one unit replacing another so that none grew too tired. As al Tarsusi said in his military manual for Saladin: *'When it is the enemy's habit to charge en bloc and to rely on the shock impact of their detachments, as do the Franks and those neighbours who resemble them, this array is very effective because if one group of enemy attacks it can be taken in the flank and surrounded.'*

On the other hand, the famous horse-archer cavalry of the Saljuq Turks suffered the most surprising reverses when pitted against early Crusader armies. By the late 11th century many Saljuq and regional armies had abandoned the old Central Asian tactics of dispersal and harassment, and reverted to time-honoured massed high-speed shooting by closely packed units of mounted bowmen. To be effective, however, this demanded a

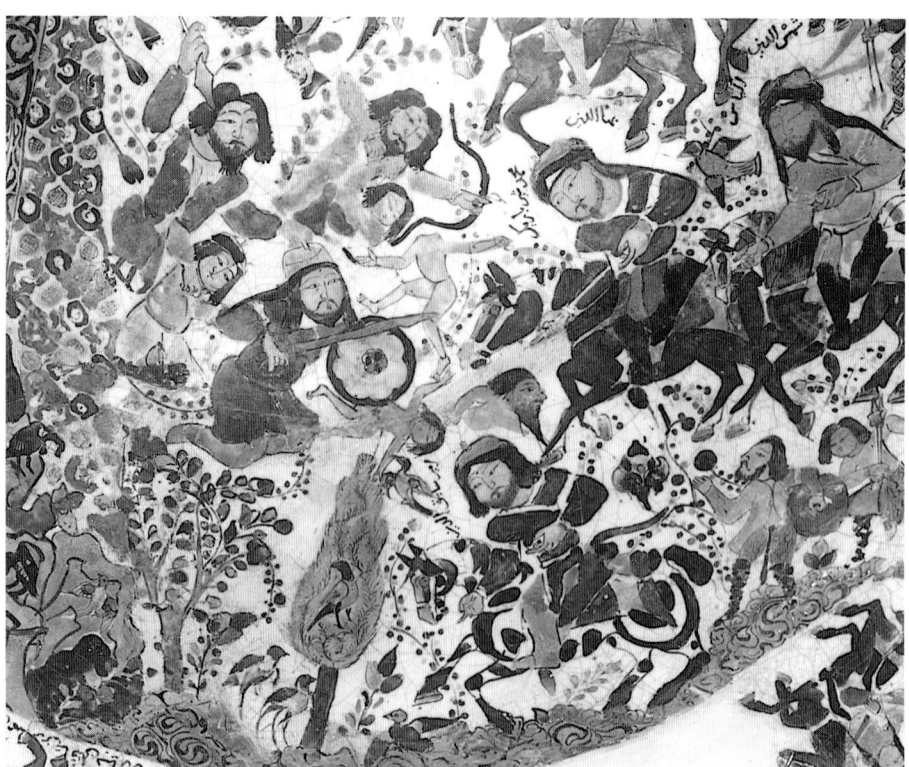

'Battle plate' from early 13th century Iran. Several members of a castle garrison emerge to challenge the attacking horsemen. (Freer Gallery of Art, inv. 43.3, Washington, USA)

very high level of training, high morale and sophisticated logistical support, particularly to keep the cavalry supplied with arrows. The success of the First Crusade probably resulted less from a superiority of European armour and tactics than from a decline in military capabilities among the fragmented Saljuq armies.

Generally speaking, one of the most important roles of later 12th and 13th century Muslim cavalry was to separate an enemy from their baggage-train, and to pen enemy infantry against an obstacle and shower them with arrows while other units dealt with enemy cavalry. Selected marksmen could harass the foe before a general engagement – as was attempted at the battle of Arsuf in 1191. Tactical manuals suggested that sharpshooters try to bring down enemy leaders. Written records also show that an enemy's communications, as well as his morale, could be undermined by shooting or otherwise overthrowing his drummers or standard-bearers.

The dramatic power of horse-archers armed with composite bows should not obscure the fact that the weapon most feared by 12th and 13th century Muslim cavalrymen was the spear; horsemen were particularly reluctant to turn their back on an enemy so armed. Unlike the almost gentlemanly jousting by knights in High Medieval Europe, the Muslim *faris* was trained to strike any vulnerable or exposed part of his enemy or his horse. Usama's *Memoires* and fictional epics in Arabic, Persian and Turkish are full of cases where men struck each other in their unarmoured legs or wounded an opponent's horse in any way possible.

If a spear broke or a man was thrown from his saddle, he usually drew his sword. The last fight of Aibak al Akrash (one of Saladin's best men) near Acre shows how a soldier would struggle on in the hope of a comrade coming to his rescue. According to Saladin's biographer, Baha al Din, Aibak's horse was killed under him so he put his back against a rock and kept the Crusaders at bay until his quiver was empty. Then he fought with his sword until finally overwhelmed by sheer numbers. Baha al Din described the death of another Muslim champion, Ayaz the Tall, later in the same campaign: '*He dismounted to pick up his lance and was trying to remount his restive horse when the Franks swooped down and killed him.*'

The death of this hero was also recorded by the

anonymous chronicler of Richard the Lionheart's Crusade, who commented on the Muslim champion's great spear: *'heavier than two of ours, to which he gave the name Aias Estog'*. One wonders how the chronicler knew. Did the wounded Ayaz speak to his enemies before he died or was one of his comrades captured? Other references indicate that swords were generally unable to penetrate armour, though they could inflict appalling injuries on unprotected parts of the body; for this reason the armour breaking mace was a popular weapon among Muslim cavalrymen.

Poets described the sound of an army at rest as like the waves of the sea, while the noise of battle consisted of the rattle of armour and harness, the clatter of swords, the crash of maces, the whistling of arrows, the twang of bows and the shouts of men. When it was all over, the men took off their armour, their eyes circled with dust, and, if victorious, set about sharing the spoils. *Ghanimah* or loot usually went to the unpaid volunteers. Other more specific, and probably more valuable, booty was divided according to a strict system of *fay*: one fifth went to the commander to cover administrative costs, and the rest went to the soldiers – more to cavalry than infantry because of their greater expenses.

In the euphoria of victory, even elite Turkish troops could revert to the pagan practice of collecting enemy heads and dangling them from the saddles of captured horses as happened after the fall of Acre in 1291. Usama mentions a short-sighted Kurdish soldier named 'Annaz who came home with his own brother Badr's head as a grisly trophy, claiming that it was a Crusader he had slain. In reality he, like others, had been beheading corpses after the battle, and once the truth was known this man fled, never to be seen again. Sometimes enemy dead were left to rot or thrown down a well and covered with lime and earth.

Wherever possible the Muslims' own dead would, of course, be given a proper burial. This was to be done on the day of death, for as the Prophet Muhammad said: *'When any one of you dies, you must not keep him in the house but carry him quickly to his grave.'* The body would be washed, its ankles or toes tied together, hands placed on the chest, wrapped in white cloth then placed in a grave on its right side with the face turned towards Mecca.

Syriac Gospels, mid-13th century, probably made in northern Iraq, showing the similarity between some Islamic military equipment and that of the European Crusaders. (Vatican Library, Ms. Syr. 559, f.135r, Rome, Italy)

Soldiers, it seemed, often carried their own shrouds on campaign.

Burial ceremonies were simple, in keeping with Islam's lack of pomp. Someone would remind the dead man's spirit of the answers he must give the angels Munkar and Nikar before entering Paradise. There were various beliefs about what happened to the dead man's soul: some said that it remained in the body until the morning after the burial; others thought that the souls of *jihad* martyrs slept in the crops of green birds which ate the fruits and drank the waters of the rivers of Paradise until the Day of Judgement.

Unlike medieval Christianity, Islam made no virtue of unnecessary suffering, and Muslim civilisation developed the most advanced medical services seen before modern times. In the Aleppo Citadel during Saladin's reign, there was a resident doctor on a fixed salary who was famous for his skill at amputations. (Generally speaking, Muslim doctors disapproved of drastic surgery unless absolutely necessary.) There was also special osteological equipment to deal with dislocated joints and

The Maristan or hospital of Nur al Din in Damascus, built in the late 12th century from the ransoms of Crusader prisoners. (Author's photograph)

fractured bones, ranging from rack-like frames for setting dislocated hips or shoulders to complex soothing ointments to reduce inflammation. Muslim doctors also performed complex operations using sophisticated surgical instruments such as saws, tongs, tweezers and drills. Cauterisation was used to remove infection around wounds, to seal amputations and to remove tumours. The religious preoccupation with cleanliness must have helped reduce the risk of infection, but Muslim doctors also inherited knowledge of medicinal drugs from the Greeks, Romans, Persians, Indians and even Chinese, as well as making their own discoveries. Usama's *Memoires* include stories of men recovering from horrific battle injuries with remarkably few cases of infection; included in these was the case of Numayr al 'Ahharuzi:

The Frank struck him with a sword on the side of his face and cut through his eyebrow, eyelid, cheek, nose and upper lip so that the whole side of his face hung down to his chest ... He arrived in Shayzar in that condition. There his face was stitched together and his cut was treated until he was healed and returned to his former condition, except that his eye was lost for good.

After a battle there would be prisoners. A strong sense of shared interest meant that captured Muslims would normally be well treated. Rulers and commanders followed the well-established tradition of generosity to defeated foes in the hope of turning them into supporters or allies. This did not normally apply to Crusader or Mongol prisoners; they would have to be ransomed if they were to escape slavery. The humiliation of prisoners was common, though mutilation was rarer. In 1157, for example, Crusader prisoners were paraded through Damascus in full armour, carrying their own flags and riding their own horses. Somewhat earlier Usama recorded how the Christians put out the right eye of a Muslim prisoner before exchanging him, so that he could not look around his shield in battle. On the Muslim side, Zangi cut off the thumbs of captured fellow-Muslim crossbowmen so that they could no longer shoot weapons that were considered particularly terrible.

ARMS & ARMOUR

Status was indicated by the quality or decoration of equipment and a man could be publicly rebuked for wearing a sword belt above his rank. Individual troops seem to have decided what their equipment should be, but they clearly had to have enough to pass muster on parade, and to be able to appear in light or full equipment depending on their duties. Elite warriors and champions had decorated arms, armour and horse harness, and guard units sometimes wore plumed head-dresses, enamelled or gilded belts, and silvered or gilded maces. Beneath such decoration Muslim cavalry kit had certain consistent features and there is little real evidence that they were lightly equipped. Indeed, Arab troops could have been mistaken for Crusaders until they were quite close. According to 12th and 13th century Syrian and Egyptian sources, basic kit was a helmet, a mail hauberk, leather or padded leggings, riding boots, sometimes spurs, a sword, a mace, an axe, a dagger, a small knife, a spear, sometimes a javelin, a shield and, for the wealthy elite, a lamellar cuirass.

Archaeological evidence suggests that one-piece iron helmets were made from the 8th century, and these may have been the *baydah* or 'egg' helmets. The earliest surviving so-called 'turban helmet' with its bulbous, pointed and often fluted shape comes from the mid-14th century but pictorial evidence from Egypt and elsewhere suggests that it was known 200 years earlier. Segmented helmets of simpler construction were used, as were leather helmets. Although the mail coif was commonplace, mail aventails attached to helmets had long been popular and were adopted in Western Europe shortly afterwards. There is also evidence of masked or visored helmets in some Turkish areas by the 13th century.

Dir or mail hauberks were usually worn beneath another garment, often two at a time. The quilted *jubbah* could contain a layer of mail the same as the hot and heavy *kazaghand*, a garment which spread to Europe as the *jazerant*. The *jawshan* or lamellar cuirass was more typical of Persian and Turkish than Arab areas, though it rose in popularity in Syria and Egypt in the 12th and 13th centuries. It could be made of hardened leather lamellae but was often of iron, clattering so loudly that it was considered unsuitable for stealthy warfare. Several references in Usama's *Memoires* show that horse-

Syriac Gospels, mid-13th century, probably made in northern Iraq. Another volume of Gospels shows soldiers wearing lamellar cuirasses. (British Library, Ms. Add. 7170, f.151r, London, England)

men took the risk of removing their armour to make themselves faster or more agile. Carelessness could also lead to injury, as when Usama's father was in such a hurry that he failed to notice that his servant had not secured one side of his *jawshan*; as a result a javelin struck him a nasty though superficial wound across the front of his chest.

The most important protection for a horseman was his shield. These varied from the large round *turs* to the elongated *tariqah* used by Crusaders, the smaller round leather *daraqah*, the spiral cane and cotton Turkish *kalkan*, the huge leather *lamt* of North Africa and the flat-based elongated 'Genoese' *januwiyah* used by infantry. In some regions shields covered in iron segments were used, but most were simply covered in leather or animal skins or painted.

The most striking offensive weapon was the re-curved composite bow. Its shape and construction gave it a draw or pull equal to that of the much larger European longbow, but it could achieve twice the range – weight for weight. Unlike the simple longbow, the wood, horn and sinew construction meant that its pull started stiff but then eased out, reducing tension as the archer took aim. It also had much greater 'potential energy' at the moment of release than a European longbow; in other words much less of its power was lost as a result of drag, friction or the inherent inflexibility of the bow itself. From the 11th century the old Hun style composite bow was gradually ousted by the newer Turkish form with its smooth rather than angled shape. This was slightly harder to draw, as it lacked some of the lever action given by the angled 'ears' of the old bow, but it gave a more efficient energy transfer when shot. It was also smaller and easier to use on horseback.

Muslim archers had developed a remarkable variety of highly specialised arrowheads for use against different targets. The 13th century *Adab al Harb'* (Art of War) by Fakhr-i Mudabbir stated that 'fish-backed' or 'ball-shaped' arrows should be used against mail or lamellar armour and most shields, the 'little spade', 'spinach', 'willow leaf', 'noodle' or 'duck's foot' against quilted soft-armour, an arrowhead of 'tempered steel' against a man in iron armour, and a 'course winged' or 'little spade' against an unprotected enemy. The rest of their equipment consisted of two spare strings for each bow and two thumb-rings for each string – more useful at long range as they tended to reduce accuracy at close range. The *nawak* arrow-guide was sometimes also used on horseback. It was a groove or channel containing a short *husban* dart the length of between a third and a hand's breadth. Groove and dart were pulled back together, and the dart was released to slide down the groove. The *nawak*'s great range and the virtual invisibility of its dart made it a useful sniper's weapon.

Almost all cavalry were armed with some form of spear, and various types of javelin were still used by fully trained cavalry in the later 13th century. A soldier's most prestigious and usually most decorated weapon was, however, his sword. Arab straight *sayf* swords descended from the Roman *gladius* continued to be used well into the 14th century – largely by infantry – as did a variety of longer straight double-edged cavalry swords. Quite when curved sabres were adopted by Muslim horsemen remains uncertain. The weapon had been developed in Central Asia by the late 8th or early 9th century and spread across most of the Muslim

Painted ceramic bowl from Raqqa, late 12th/early 13th century. Everything about the rider's equipment is typically Islamic except for his Byzantine-style shield. (Staatliche Museum, Berlin, Germany)

Arab cavalryman, early 12th century (See text commentary for detailed captions)

A

B

The charge of Yaqut the Tall

C

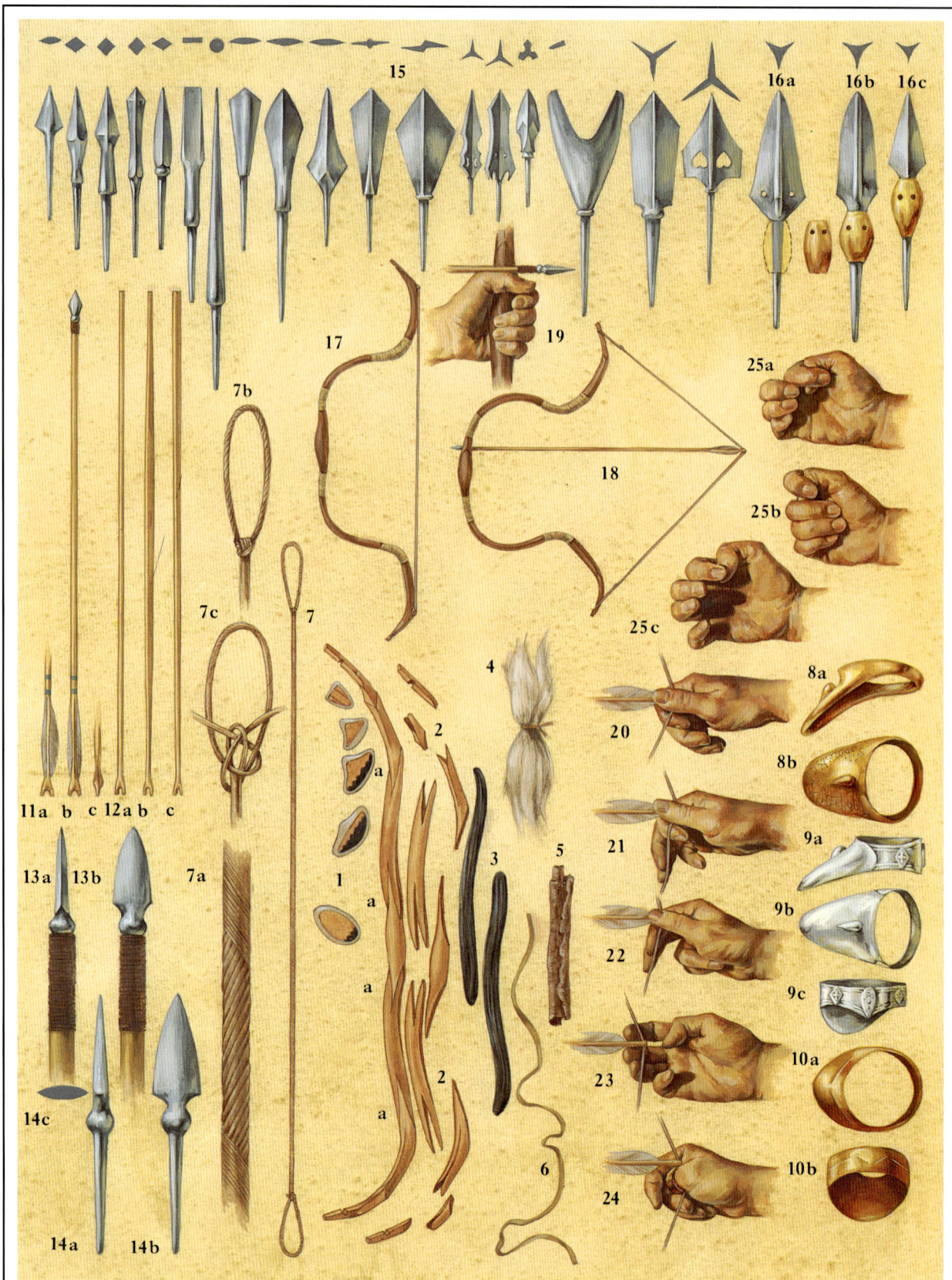

D Archery equipment (See text commentary for detailed captions)

Muslim horse-archers in action

F: Turkish cavalryman, late 12th century (See text commentary for detailed captions)

Treating the wounded

H

Horse harness (See text commentary for detailed captions)

I   Muslim male costume (See text commentary for detailed captions)

Usama ibn Munqidh in retirement

K   Persian cavalryman, early 13th century (See text commentary for detailed captions)

world in the wake of Turkish mercenaries, slave-warriors and conquerors. It remained more characteristic of Turkish troops than of their Persian, Kurdish or Arab comrades for several centuries.

Maces had been used for several centuries and those mentioned in Fatimid sources were up to 1 m long. Al Tarsusi's treatise on weaponry lists various types, some made entirely of iron, others with an iron or bronze head that was 'toothed', flanged, smooth, cucumber shaped or consisted of rings. The mace seems to have had almost mystical significance for the Turks, probably stemming from the ancient Turkish paganism. The full equipment of a mid-13th century Turkish champion was described in the *Danishmandname* by 'Arif 'Ali Toqati:

*First of all he dressed in an embroidered shirt
which was embroidered with gold.
Over this shirt he put on a coat of mail
in which the links were of gold or were riveted with gold.
At his waist he belted a sword, a precious gift
which even the Shah of Kashmir had not seen even in a dream.
He belted on also a quiver, Oh my beloved,
one which only the Khakhan* [pre-Islamic Turkish emperor of Central Asia] *had power to see.
Next he placed his mace in its holder
and on his arm he put a Chinese shield.
In his hand he put a spear so sharp that
if it struck an enemy it shattered him to pieces.*

The dagger was a more prosaic weapon, though regarded as versatile and as a last line of defence. The large *khanjar* was the most common and the slender *yafrut* was used only by Berbers. The standard cavalry axe was the *tabarzin* or 'saddle axe'. Other types, for use on horseback or on foot, were the *najikh*, which had a point or hammer at the back, and the somewhat obscure *durbash*. Tribal Turks and invading Mongols used lassos, and these were greatly feared even by highly trained professional Muslim cavalry.

Horse armour was known to Muslim cavalry during the early medieval and Crusader period and seems to have been more widely used than in Europe, at least until the 13th century. Early horse

Bronze plaque of 13th century Iran illustrating Bahram Gur, 'The Mighty Hunter', and his singing girl. (Private collection)

armours were usually called *tijfaf*, a word that reflected their felt construction though some incorporated mail, lamellar or scale defences as well as rigid protections for the horse's head.

Manufacture & Maintenance of Equipment

The main arms industries of the Muslim world were located in forested regions on its fringes, close to iron mining areas; most were far from the main centres of population and military power, but the great cities of the Middle East had arms bazaars where soldiers could buy equipment or have damaged kit repaired. Major campaigns led to acute shortages, with agents trying to buy weaponry far afield, and armourers at home working overtime. Great efforts were also made to recover the equipment of dead enemies. Usama described one of his *kazaghands* as being made from two mail hauberks, the longer one being of Crusader origin, the shorter of Muslim manufacture.

The military challenge of the Crusades, along

Painted paper from Fustat. Fatimid from the 11th/12th century. This damaged fragment shows a turbaned horseman wearing a lamellar cuirass that seems to include arm defences, perhaps over a mail hauberk. (Private collection)

five spans long, and the broader *salmani*, four fingers wide and four spans long. A surviving 9th–11th century sabre excavated at Nishapur in Iran is, in fact, 3.5 cm (two fingers) wide and 71.5 cm (three and a half spans) long excluding the lost hilt.

Sword typologies also dealt with materials and whether they had been forged from a single ingot, built up of layers, cast in a mould or cut from a sheet. European swords were pattern-welded from hard but brittle 'male' iron. More flexible Asiatic blades of *fuladh* steel were made from soft 'female' iron treated and forged in various ways.

The first forging was done at a much higher temperature than was possible in Europe, being nearer to white-hot than merely red. Blades were then beaten from the steel compounds, and the resulting weapons were characterised by a beautiful surface pattern called *firind* – now known as 'watering'. Surviving examples contain much cementite (iron carbide) which makes metal hard but brittle. Other chemicals were also added during a process of alternate heatings and quenchings, and the result was a blade with the hardest metal along the cutting edge but which was also astonishingly flexible and virtually unbreakable.

Making of a complete sword and its accoutrements required the skills of a smelter, a forger, a smith, a temperer or sharpener, a hilt maker and fixer, a scabbard wood shaper, a tanner for the leather covering of the scabbard, a scabbard ornamenter, a chape-maker and a belt stitcher – probably in some sort of production-line. Indeed, surviving bronze matrices for making moulds to mass-produce parts of the hilt and scabbard have been found.

The manufacture of the composite bow was almost as complicated as that of a sword-blade. Various stages were influenced by the weather, and it could take one or two years to complete. Different types of wood, glue, horn and sinew were used in different regions, depending upon their availability and the climate in which the bow was used. For example, Far Eastern bowyers used bamboo wood, spinal sinew and fish glue; Central Asians ramhorn, Indians and Middle Easterners water-buffalohorn and sinews from an animal's Achilles tendon. Bows also came in different sizes and strengths depending on whether the weapon was for hunting,

with the willingness of Islamic civilisation to learn and experiment, led to some strange weapons being invented, though most did not get beyond the prototype stage. Al Tarsusi in his book on weapons refers to several weird ideas, ranging from crossbows fixed inside shields to multiple crossbows inside revolving wooden frames. Some of these ideas resurfaced in southern Spain and Venice a century or so later.

Arab, Persian and Turkish smiths used early forms of decarbonised steel for their best helmets, swords and spears. There was a passionate interest in sword typology; scholars drew up complicated family trees to illustrate the relationship between various forms. The slender *qala'i* blade, for example, was two and a half fingers wide and four to

training or war. The 13th century *Adab al Harb* described the widely used Khwarazmi bow from Central Asia as having a short limb and long ear, and a thick bow-string of horse-hide. It was considered inaccurate and wobbly. The Parvanchi, Ghaznachi, Karuri and Lawhuri bows of Afghanistan and Pakistan were preferred by marksmen.

Most arrows were made from poplar or willow, the former being heavy for short range, the latter light for long range. Arrows made wholly or partly of reed gave the greatest range of all. Since arrowheads were of the tanged type a hole had to be bored in the shaft unless it was of reed. One 13th century archery text specifies that a man's arrows should be as long as the distance between the top of his shoulder to the tip of his middle finger, or from armpit to the tip of the forefinger, or from elbow to elbow when the fists were held together.

Al Tarsusi's book on late 12th century weaponry gives instructions on how to make hardened leather *jawshans* and *khud* helmets. Contrary to popular opinion, hardened leather was not 'boiled in oil', which would simply have made it softer, but was treated in oil before being shaped in a mould where it was probably hardened and waterproofed with wax. Leather armours also lent themselves to decorative gilding.

Ordinary soldiers were responsible for the maintenance, repair and appearance of their kit; a man was expected to clean his mail in a noxious but effective mixture of ash, dung and oily sediment. He also attended to the rawhide or silk lacing system of his lamellar cuirass, checking for any rot, wear or holes and fixing minor problems himself.

Museums, Collections and Collecting

Muslims did not place artefacts in the graves of their dead. The Middle East has suffered many invasions that have destroyed or dispersed treasured relics, and modern archaeology has only recently begun to study Islamic civilisation in detail. Consequently very little arms and armour survives from the medieval Middle East, and much of what does exist is in private collections. Where illustrated manuscripts and other pictorial sources are concerned, Western domination of the Muslim world during the 19th and early 20th centuries meant that many of the greatest libraries were pillaged. As a result, with a few notable exceptions, the finest collections are now in Europe, Russia and North America.

(* Collection of primary importance; ** Worth a special journey. Note that non-military objects are included as sources of pictorial information.)

Armenia
Yerevan: Matendarian Library (manuscripts)*

Egypt
Cairo: Bab al Nasr city gate (carvings)*
Museum of Islamic Art (wood-carving, manuscript fragments, ceramics, metalwork, ivories, textiles, arms, armour, clothing)**

12th/13th century painted paper charm showing the devil armed with a curved sword and riding an elephant. It was found in the ruins of Fustat on the outskirts of Cairo. (British Museum, London, England)

France
Paris: Bibliothèque Nationale (manuscripts, ivories, metalwork, coins)**
Musée du Louvre (ceramics, metalwork, stucco, ivories, wood-carvings, stone-carvings, manuscript fragments, arms, armour)**

Germany
Berlin: Staatliche Museum Dahlem (ivories, metalwork, ceramics, stucco, armour)*

Iran
Isfahan: Archaeological Museum (archer's thumb-rings)
Tehran: Iran Bastan Museum (ceramics, wall-painting, metalwork, arms, horse harness)*

Iraq
Baghdad: National Museum (carved gateway)
Mosul: Church of Mar Hudeni (carvings)*

Israel and Palestine
Jerusalem: Syrian Orthodox Convent of St. Mark Library (manuscripts)
Franciscan Museum (grenades)
Rockefeller Museum (ceramics, manuscript fragments)

Italy
Florence: Museo Nazionale di Bargello (ivories, metalwork)
Palermo: Cappella Palatina (painted ceiling panels)*
Rome: Istituto di Studi Medievale Orientale (ceramics)

Russia
Moscow: State Historical Museum (arms, armour)*
St. Petersburg: State Hermitage Museum (ivories, metalwork, ceramics, stone carvings, arms, armour, horse harness, textiles, clothing)**
Oriental Institute, Russian Academy of Sciences (manuscripts)*

Syria
Damascus: National Museum (ceramics, armour)*

Turkey
Bodrum: Castle Museum (arms)*
Istanbul: Army Museum (arms, armour)**
Museum of Turkish and Islamic Art (metalwork, war drum, stucco, stone carvings)**
Süleymaniye Library (manuscripts)*
Topkapi Museum (arms, metalwork, ceramics, coins)**

Despite the rapid pace of modernisation in the Middle East, some traditional forms of house still exist. Domed clay buildings, like these north of the Syrian city of Hama, are clearly shown in 13th century manuscripts. Then as now they were inhabited by poorer people, including ordinary soldiers and the tenants of more successful cavalry officers. (Author's photograph)

Northern Syria was a land of cities, peasant villages, semi-nomadic trans-humants and nomads from the deep desert. Tented rather than settled peoples provided the bulk of troops. They and their families, like the Arab Bedouin seen here beside the river Orontes near Jisr al Shugur in Syria, would have migrated according to the seasons. (Author's photograph)

Left: Turcoman nomad encampment near Nigde in central Turkey. During the 12th century Turks came to dominate the ruling elites and most armies of the Middle East. (Author's photograph)

Topkapi Library (manuscripts)**
Van area: Aght'amar island, Church of Gagik (relief carvings)*

United Kingdom
London: British Library (manuscripts)**
British Museum (metalwork, ceramics, ivories, arms, manuscript fragments)*
Tower of London (swords)
Victoria and Albert Museum (metalwork, ceramics, ivories, glassware, textiles, arms)**
Oxford: Bodleian Library (manuscripts)

United States of America
Boston: Museum of Fine Art (manuscripts, ceramics, metalwork, textiles, stucco)*
Los Angeles: County Museum of Art (arms)
New York: Brooklyn Museum (manuscripts, ceramics)
Metropolitan Museum of Art (glass, ceramics, metalwork, ivories, stucco, manuscripts, stone carving, wall paintings, arms, horse harness)**
Pierpoint Morgan Library (manuscripts)*
Washington: Freer Gallery of Art (ceramics, metalwork, manuscripts)**
Textile Museum (textiles)

Vatican City
Vatican Library (manuscripts)*

THE PLATES

A: Arab cavalryman, early 12th century
1 Archetypal Arab. The most important characteristics are the turban, here worn over an imported Italian helmet, and the fact that he is protected by a mail hauberk rather than lamellar armour. In many ways he had more in common with southern European warriors than those from the eastern Islamic lands. *2* Embroidered edging and block-printed pattern of cotton tunic. *3* The *dir'* mail hauberk. The main difference between this and a European hauberk was the opening at the neck and the raised collar stiffened by leather thongs. *3a* The best Middle Eastern mail consisted of alternating riveted and punched links. *3b* Detail of rawhide stiffening of the collar. *4* Italian one-piece helmet with inlaid gold decoration on the top and a gilded bronze strip around the rim. Southern European helmets, presumably also those exported to Egypt, differed from northern European forms in several respects, above all in the number of vertical 'keels' indicating greater strength at the front and sides. *5* Bronze war-hammer with silver decoration. The hook at the back may have been designed to pull an enemy from his horse. The wooden haft with its leather-bound grip and wrist strap are based on written descriptions. *6* Exploded view of a straight-bladed Arab *sayf* sword with a bronze pommel and quillons, and a leather-covered wooden grip. The 'sleeve' beneath the quillons would have enclosed the top of the sword's scabbard, protecting the blade from dust or rain. *6a* Fully assembled sword. *7* Rear and side views of a wooden *turs* shield; the front is covered with leather. Two leather grip-straps are attached to rings inside four of the six external rivets.

B: A lion hunt
'*All of a sudden we were surprised to see the lion rush past us like the wind and go straight to one of our comrades named Sa'dallah al Shaybani and knock his horse to the ground with one blow. I thrust my lance into the lion, hitting it in the middle part of its body, and it died on the spot.*' (Memoires, Usama Ibn Munqidh)

Hunting served as a highly realistic form of military

'Rabi Ibn Adnan attacks his enemies by night' in this 13th century Warqa wa Gulshah manuscript, probably painted in what is now eastern Turkey or north-western Iran. Rabi and a companion are shown as armoured cavalrymen wearing lamellar jawshan cuirasses. They are supported by infantrymen with kite-shaped shields. (Topkapi Lib., Ms. Haz 841, f.6a, Istanbul, Turkey)

training in the Middle East, just as it did in medieval Europe. Lions and other wild cats still roamed Syria and Egypt in the 12th century, and hunting them could be very dangerous. Not only did it require courage and skill with weapons, but also great control over the huntsman's often terrified horse. The lion also had to be tracked and trapped before being killed with a spear or sword. Other forms of hunting included hawking – perhaps the most 'aristocratic' sport – and chasing the deer and wild asses of the desert. Usama's *Memoires* devote almost as much time to these pastimes, and the sometimes extraordinary adventures of the huntsmen, as to recollections of war.

C: The charge of Yaqut the Tall

'*Yaqut the Tall swerved and turned back against his pursuers, as my father and my uncle were watching him. He struck a horseman who was riding next to another man, pursuing our people. Both horsemen and horses fell to the ground ... This soldier was addicted to making money illegally and to other wrong deeds, but every time my father wanted to discipline Yaqut my uncle would say; "Brother, forgive him for my sake and don't forget that lance thrust."*' (Memoires, Usama Ibn Munqidh)

According to Usama, this incident occurred in one of the many minor skirmishes along the frontiers between the Crusader states and their Muslim neighbours. The two Crusaders probably failed to notice Yaqut until the last moment. Such clashes took a small but steady toll of life on both sides, yet they almost seem to have been seen as a rough form of warrior 'sport' rather than a serious *jihad* or Crusade. Most clashes in Usama's *Memoires* involve the use of spears or swords in combat rather than horse-archery.

D: Archery equipment

1 Assembled bow shown without its bark covering. *1a* Four stress points. These would be bound with rawhide. *2* Nine pieces of wood forming the body of the bow. *3* Two pieces of black horn, straightened before use, with ridged interiors to help the glue stick. *4* Strands of sinew. *5* A roll of birch-bark for use as a covering around the bow. *6* Rawhide to be bound around the stress points (*1a*). *7* Complete

Carved ivory plaque, Fatimid Egypt or Iraq, 11th–12th century. Not all hunting was done on horseback, even by the cavalry elite. (Bargello Museum, Florence, Italy)

bowstring. *7a* Detail of bowstring showing the cotton-thread covering. *7b–c* Knotted loop (tight and loosened) at each end of the bowstring. *8a–b* Bronze thumb-ring with a Farsi inscription. *9a–c* Silver thumb-ring. *10a–b* Bronze thumb-ring with simple decoration. *11a–c* A complete arrow showing fletching and nock. *12a* 'Straight hewn' arrow shaft. *12b* 'Barley grain' arrow shaft. *12c* 'Candle form' arrow shaft. *13a–b* Face and side views of an arrowhead with its binding. *14a–c* Side, face and sectional views of arrowhead. *15* Various forms of iron arrowheads. *16a–c* Arrowheads with bronze 'whistles'. *17* Composite bow at rest. *18* Composite bow at full draw. *19* Left hand gripping the bow with the arrow to the right of the bow. *20* Primary release. *21* Secondary release. *22* Tertiary release. *23* Mediterranean release. *24* 'Thumb draw' or Mongolian release using a thumb-ring. *25a–c* Variations on the 'thumb draw'.

Kitab al Tiryaq, 'Book of Antidotes'. Made in Mosul c. AD1250. Huntsmen career along the top register while a caravan fills the lower panel. In the middle a prince watches a man cook kebabs. (Nationalbibliothek, Ms. AF.10, Vienna, Austria)

E: Muslim horse-archers in action

'If you wish to shoot and have a sword, drop the sword from your right hand, seize the wrist loop and slide it up the right forearm. Hold the bow and three arrows in your left hand. If you are on horseback and are also armed with a lance, push the lance beneath the right thigh. If you have a sword as well, put the lance beneath the left thigh. If a group of enemy halt out of range, disperse to shoot at them. If they come close, reassemble your forces. If you are near the enemy on a road, regroup to keep him on your left.' [Murda al Tarsusi, Book of Military Equipment and Tactics written for Saladin]

Documentary sources show that Muslim horse-archers used a variety of tactics including 'shower shooting' at a designated area or 'killing zone' rather than at an individual enemy. This was an essentially

Persian tactic originally designed to cope with Turkish raiders from the Central Asian steppes in pre-Islamic times. The other most important form of horse-archery was Turkish in origin and involved shooting while the horse was in motion, either harassing an enemy from a distance or repeatedly charging and shooting. The aim was to get close, shoot at a range where the arrow would pierce almost any form of protection, then retreat out of range of counter-fire.

F: Turkish cavalryman, late 12th century

1 This figure has been given as many Turkish items of clothing and equipment as possible. He also wears his hair in the long plaited pigtail typical of tribal Turks. He wields a *latt* form of mace. The sabre was often carried using what would later be known in Europe as the Italian Grip, with the forefinger over the quillons. **1a** Detail of motif from woodblock printed cotton sash around waist. **1b** Printed motif from cotton trousers. **2a–d** Hypothetical exploded view of a *sharbush* hat based on later traditional headgear. Sewn segments of stiV felt with the upturned brim pronounced at the front (**2a**). Covering in red silk (**2b**) with a yellow silk 'button' on top. Fur lining (**2c**) only covering the brim. Peak decorated with a gilded and tooled leather 'plate' (**2d**). **3** Interior of the shield showing the padded leather squab plus grip-straps and a long guige to go around the neck. **4a** Front view of the iron lamellar cuirass, laced to a felt jacket. **4b** Rear view of the cuirass. **4c** Detail of the interior of the jacket. **4d** Three views of a single iron lame. **4e** One simple version of lacing a lamellar cuirass using three laces for every row. The lower edging is here covered with a narrow strip of leather. **5a** Decorated outer face of scabbard for a slightly curved sabre, without its bronze suspension points and chape. **5b** Interior of one half of the scabbard. The outside would have a raised decoration, probably of gesso. **5c** Sectional view of scabbard. **5d** Fine leather covering for scabbard. **5e** Undecorated inner face of the scabbard, with stitching to secure the leather covering. **5f–h** Exterior, sectional view and interior of one bronze suspension point. These consisted of two pieces riveted together. **5i–k** Exterior, section and bottom view of the bronze chape. This also consisted of two pieces of metal, apparently soldered together. **6a** The blade of a slightly curved sabre. **6b–c** Two halves of the wooden grip secured to the tang of the blade by rivets. **6d** The upper rivet also secured a small bronze plate and a ring to which a wrist strap could be attached. **6e–g** Inner, outer and sectional views of cast bronze quillons. These again consisted of two pieces of metal apparently soldered together. **7** Exploded view of a *latt* form of mace, with a cast bronze head and wooden haft. **8** Exploded and whole views of soft leather riding boots. These were buckled to a narrow belt beneath the tunic. **9** Iron dagger and sheath worn in leg of right boot.

G: Treating the wounded

'When they came near us I saw that the man in the middle had been struck across the centre of his face by a Crusader's sword . . . One half of his face was so loose that it hung over his chest and between the two halves was a gap almost the width of a hand-span . . . The surgeon sewed his face and treated it. The sides stuck together and the man recovered . . . He used to deal in

Crossbow mounted inside a shield. The crossbow incorporates an angled composite bow. (Bodleian Lib., Ms. Hunt 264, f.117, Oxford, England)

beasts of burden and was thereafter nicknamed Ibn Ghazi The Slashed One.' [*Memoires,*Usama Ibn Munqidh]

Muslim troops were fortunate in having far better medical backup than their Crusader opponents. Medicaments were mostly based on herbal extracts and distilled natural oils. Doctors or surgeons were highly respected professionals whose services were also in demand from the Crusader enemy. In fact the revival of medical science in Western Europe, Wrstly in Italy and Spain, owed more to what these countries learned from their Muslim neighbours across the Mediterranean than to any rediscovery of forgotten Roman or Greek medical knowledge.

H: Horse harness

1 Arab horse harness developed from a fusion of the Bedouin style and the traditions of the Mediterranean and Sassanian Iran. It was associated with what has become known as 'The High Islamic Riding School' which in turn contributed to medieval, Renaissance and modern European riding styles. *1a* Detail of pattern from thick woven woollen saddle blanket. *2* Bronze harness pendant. *3* Bronze bridle attachment. *4* Bronze trefoil strap linkage. *5* A complete bridle consisting of leather cheek, brow, neck and chin straps, a broadened nose band covered with a panel of embroidered silk, a bronze curb bridle and a twisted scarf. *6* The wooden saddle frame or 'tree' had a broad strap supporting the seat, two leather-padded wooden panels on each side of the horse's spine, and attachments for breast and crupper-straps, and for girth and stirrup leathers. *6a* Rear view of the cantle showing the 'tunnel' beneath the seat. *7* Complete saddle with partial leather covering. Padded seat, tooled leather or embroidered fabric flaps, canvas girth, knotted stirrup leathers and bronze stirrups. *8* The Turkish tribal horse harness was simpler. Here the saddle is removed but a shaped horse blanket is held in place by a secondary girth. The knotted tail and neck tassel are typically Turkish. *8a* Simple Turkish bridle consisting of plain leather straps and an iron snaffle bit with long cheek-pieces or psalions. Separate leather collar decorated with pierced bronze medallions and a henna-stained horsehair tassel in a bronze holder. *8b* Top view of the hinged mouth piece. *8c* Detail of bronze buckle. *8d* Detail of a bronze collar medallion. *9* The wood-framed saddle was basically the same as that in the Arab saddle, though the pommel was typically tilted forward. *9a* Rear view of cantle. *9b* Front view of pommel. *9c* Basic saddle with rounded leather skirt and cloth-covered leather flap. *9d* Complete saddle including quilted

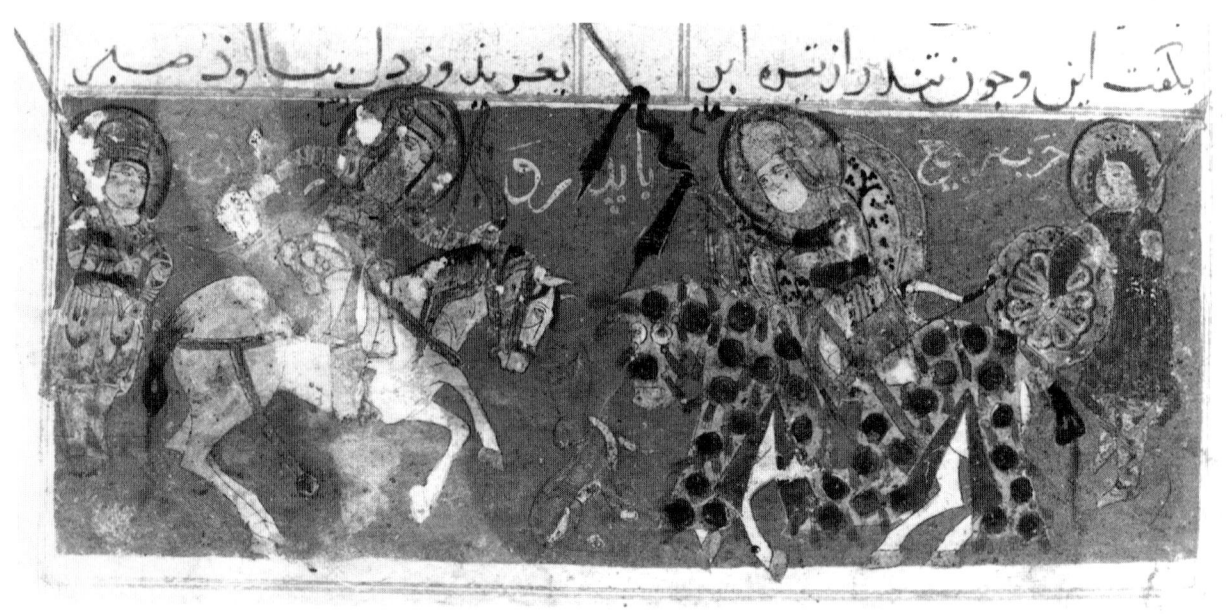

'Rabi Ibn Adnan fights Warqa's father.' The young Rabi appears as an armoured horse archer (left) while Warqa's aged father (right) is a white-bearded lancer riding a fully caparisoned horse. (Topkapi Lib., Ms. Haz 841, f.15a, Istanbul, Turkey)

fabric seat, decorative cloth panels front and rear, plain leather breast- and breeching straps. *9e* Detailed front and side views of silver-inlaid bronze stirrups for use with soft riding boots. *9f* Detail of pierced bronze medallion used as a harness or breeching-strap linkage.

I: Muslim male costume
1 Muslim costume was essentially functional rather than ceremonial. Through changing fashions the basic garments remained the same. Here a man wears the first layer of clothing: a *qayah* satin skull cap (*1a*), *tubban* drawers and *jurab* cotton stockings. *1b Tubban* drawers laid flat with the draw-string loosened. *2* Muslim garments were very loose-

Below: The military history of Cairo is summed up in this photograph taken from the Muqattam Hill. Closest to the camera is 'The Army Mosque' built for Badr al Jamali, the Armenian commander-in-chief of the Fatimid armies in AD1085 and is still within a prohibited military compound. Beyond stands the great Cairo Citadel built for Saladin. (Author's photograph)

Right: The Bakrwali House, Rashid, Egypt. Until the late 12th century almost all Egyptian buildings were of brick. No medieval houses survive but a few similar early 19th century examples have been restored in the picturesque backwater of Rashid. (Author's photograph)

fitting; the normal width of a loom was 70 cm. This was also true of the *qamis* or shirt where the sleeves were attached at right angles to the body. *3 Sirwal* or quilted woollen trousers worn by soldiers in cold weather. The crotch was extremely wide – remarkably comfortable in hot or sweaty weather. *4 Qaba* silk tunic or coat. The front is asymmetrical, the right side is cut at an angle and overlaps the left which is cut vertically. *4a Tiraz* or bands were almost invariably sewn adjacent to the shoulder-hole of the body. The very full lower part of the *qaba* has three additional panels at each side. *4b* Fabric button and loop to secure neck. The waist would have been secured by a belt. *5* Persian-style woollen *qaftan*, based on an example excavated at Moschevaya Balka in the Caucasus. It is a complex garment, made of numerous panels. The sleeves are narrower than garments seen in the Arab countries. *6* A heavy woollen *durra'ah*; the kind of garment worn during cold weather by Arab peoples since pre-Islamic times. The seams of the sleeves are along the top of the arms, whereas on Persian and Turkish tunics they were along the bottom. Each seam is decorated with strips of plain embroidery (*6a*). The *tiraz* bands (*6b*) around the sleeve have no dedicatory inscription. The *durra'ah* was put on over the head; hence the similarities drawn by Arab writers between the mail *dir'* hauberk and the *durra'ah* tunic – both names having the same origin in Arabic. *7 Jubbah*, a coat of fur-lined satin. The embroidered *tiraz* panels are unusual in being attached further down the sleeve than was normal. The garment opens fully down the front and seems to have no fasteners. A great variety of head-gear was seen in the medieval Muslim world. It indicated an individual's origin, religion, status and role. *8a* Almost all were worn over a simple *qayah* skull-cap, like the one just visible beneath this Turkish soft felt *qub* cap. *8b Qalansuwa tawila* or 'tall qalansuwa' of cloth over a wickerwork or straw frame. *8c* Probably a *qalansuwa shashiya*, a style which originated in Transoxania. It was a quilted hat of several segments, stuffed with coarse material and covered in silk. *8d* The *imamah* form of turban was seen through the Arab world and beyond. It was wound round a small *qalansuwah* hat – just visible on top. *8e* The *imamah adhahaba* was wound in higher shape than the ordinary turban. Here the ends of the turban-cloth hang loose to form a *rafraf*. *8f* The *imamah muhannak* or 'hanging' turban had one length of cloth going under the chin. It remained fashionable in North Africa and among the Arab Bedouin. It was also worn by some senior religious figures, though their turbans were fuller and larger than here. *9* Thick *ra'n* or gaiters of strong cloth stuffed with cotton waste and edged with strips of leather. This Persian form of protection for a horseman's legs would be worn over *khuff* boots. *10* Soft leather *khuff* boots without gaiters. The uppers were made of three pieces of soft leather with the soles wrapped slightly up the sides. *10a* The back had a short slit which could be laced tight. *11 Muza* or tight-fitting Persian riding boots. Manuscripts usually show the knee panel in a

A Muslim revival was the driving force behind resistance to the Crusaders. It was centred upon the ancient university-mosque of al Azhar in Cairo founded in AD970. (Author's photograph)

lighter colour, probably indicating that it was of softer leather. This was buckled to a waist belt. *12* Sturdy Arab *na'l* or leather sandals have been worn by desert peoples since ancient times. Written evidence suggests that the military form of *na'l*, as used by Arab infantry, had much in common with those once worn by Roman legionaries. The soles could also be of woven palm-fibre. *13 Madan* slipper-shoes would have been worn in the city or indoors, though people would remove their footwear before entering the private parts of a house. Such slippers were often decorated with bright fabric.

J: Usama ibn Munqidh in retirement

'Be young while you can, but when you reach old age act like an elder for then youthful conduct would be undignified. Anyone who acts like a young man in his older years is like someone who sounds the trumpet for a charge during a retreat . . . Be kinder to the old than to the young, for youth still has hope of growing old whereas old age has nothing to expect but death.' [Kai Ka'us Ibn Iskandar, Prince of Gurgan, Book of Advice written for his son, late 11th century]

Hama and the Orontes in Syria, with the striped minaret of the Mosque of Nur an Din, built in AD1172, overlooking the river. (Author's photograph)

A successful soldier could retire in respect and perhaps prosperity. Those that survived could also hope to reach a good age as the diet and more hygienic conditions of medieval Islamic culture seem to have led to a longer life-span than was normal in Europe. Many men from the educated elite took up writing or teaching, often having written a fair amount of poetry while serving as soldiers, just as Usama did. Others seem to have trained younger soldiers or took up civilian careers as merchants. Business and trade were perfectly honourable professions; the profit motive was not seen in the same dubious light as it was in Christian Europe. Usama wears long, full clothes, a shawl and large turban; these are associated with old age – which was greatly respected in Islamic civilisation.

K: Persian cavalryman, early 13th century

1 Persian warriors had their own traditions which

The Bayad wa Riyad *manuscript, Morocco or Andalusia, early 13th century. Music and poetry played a crucial role in the life of medieval Muslim civilisation. (Vatican Library, Ms. Ar. 368, Rome, Italy)*

seem to have included the covering of helmets with fabric caps and the use of mail-lined, cloth-covered armours. The shaft of this man's spear is hollow (*a*), made of two halves glued together and bound with strips of fabric. *2a–d* The cloth-covered helmet had a basic fluted iron protection (*a*) with a small vent on top. A lined mail aventail was attached by a wire threaded through the mail links and the turned lower rim of the helmet (*b*). The helmet and part of the aventail were covered by a silk-covered felt hat (*c*) made in sections rather like the *qalansuma shashiya*. The lining of the helmet probably consisted of a laced leather crown (*d*) riveted to the interior of the rim. *3* Few fragments of medieval Persian lamellar armour have been found, and none retains its original lacing. The reconstruction shown here is based on evidence from neighbouring regions. The complete *jawshan* cuirass consisted of rows of lamellae laced to each other vertically and horizontally, secured over the shoulders by buckled straps and buckled at the back. *3a* Detailed view of the interior of the cuirass; more of the lacing was exposed here than on the front. *3b* A single iron lame. *3c* Small section of the cuirass 'stretched' to show how the lacing system may have worked – similar to that used in Tibet and south-western China until the 19th century. Each lame had two vertical and three horizontal laces passing through it. The best Middle Eastern lamellar appeared to have had silk lacing which was less susceptible to rot than leather. *4* A partially 'exploded' view of mail-lined *kazaghand* armour. It looked like an ordinary coat except for its raised collar where the mail was stiffened in the same way as in an ordinary *dir'* hauberk. The *kazaghand* was also characterised by numerous rivets across its surface to secure the various layers. The innermost was made of heavy cotton padded with rabbit's skin. Next comes the first layer of mail – in this instance a long-hemmed long-sleeved hauberk captured from the Crusaders, then a layer of quilted cotton filled with silk waste. This *kazaghand* is based on one described in Usama's *Memoires*. The second layer of mail has a short-hemmed short-sleeved mail hauberk of Islamic origin. Over this was the outer layer of silk brocade. The *kazaghand* opened fully down the front where there was an overlap. A slit at the back of the garment went from hem to crotch. *4a* Detail of one silvered bronze rivet surrounded by six small 'dots' of silver thread. *4b* Detail of one of the substantial silver thread loops and silver thread-covered wooden buttons. *4c* Position of *tiraz* bands around sleeves, if worn. *5a* Small riding boot of soft leather with a rawhide sole drawn slightly up the sides of the shoe. A loop at the back helped the wearer pull on the boot. *5b* Heavy rawhide gaiter with fabric rosettes sewn to each side, leather edging and laces to tie the gaiter at the back of the leg. *6* Silver-inlaid iron *tabarzin* or cavalry axe. *7* For many years the idea that metal shields were used before the 15th century was dismissed as unrealistic. Recently such a shield was found in a medieval Islamic site in Transoxania and is reconstructed here. The leaf-like iron segments and iron rim are attached to an ordinary wooden shield and have a leather edging. A highly decorated bronze boss is based on what was probably a number of thin shield-bosses from Iran and Afghanistan. There may have been a decorative outer boss (*a*) riveted to a substantial iron inner boss (*b*), the rivet having a washer (*c*). The grip shown on the inner view (*d*) is based on surviving medieval shields from Spain. It is made of a wooden bar nailed across the entire parchment-covered inner surface, and its curved grip area is covered in leather. The bar is also secured by a pair of bronze staples. Inside the shield-boss has been padded and given a leather covering to protect the hand. The edge of the hole in the wooden shield has also been edged with leather. *7e* Sectional view of complete shield. *7f* Side view of complete shield.

Glossary

'Asabiyah – tribal solidarity
'Askar – a ruler's personal regiments
Coif – flexible head-protection
Composite bow – bow made of wood, horn and sinew
Dir' – mail hauberk (armour)
Faris – cavalryman
Furusiya – cavalry skills
Halqa – elite regiments of the Ayyubid army
Hauberk – mail body-armour

Fortified walls of Cairo just east of the Bab Zuwayla gate, almost smothered by today's houses and tenements. (Author's photograph)

Hujra – barracks
'Iqta – fief
'Istina' – obligation between soldier and patron
Jamakiya – military pay
Jawshan – lamellar body armour
Jaysh – army in general
Jihad – religious struggle, including war
Jubbah – mail-lined armour
Jund – originally a militia army, later the Ayyubid military elite
Kazaghand – mail-lined armour
Lamellar – armour of rigid pieces laced together
Mamluk – soldier of slave origin
Mawali – honorary member of Arab tribe
Maydan – parade ground
Tawashi – elite professional cavalryman
Turcoman – Turkish tribal nomad
Zardkhanah – arsenal

Bibliography

The following list does not include contemporary chronicles which can be found in any bibliography of the Crusades. Untranslated Arabic, Persian and Turkish sources have also been omitted.

B.J. Beshir, 'Fatimid Military Organization', *Der Islam* LV (1978)

A. Bombaci, 'The Army of the Saljuqs of Rum',

Above: Carved stucco decoration over the entrance portal of the prayer hall in the University Mosque of al Azhar in Cairo, c. AD1130. The richest or most successful professional soldiers would retire to live in luxury but to get an idea of their highly decorated houses one must look at surviving buildings, almost all of which are religious. (Author's photograph)

Left: Two members of the Saljuq Turkish cavalry elite. One carries a shield, the other a spear. Shown on a 13th century glazed tile from Iran. The rider on the right appears to be wearing a double-pointed dushakh *hat (Mus. of Oriental Art, Inv. 1056, Rome, Italy*

Istituto orientale di Napoli, Annali n.s. XXXVIII (1978)

H. Derenbourg, *Ousama Ibn Mounkidh, un Emir Syrien au Premier Siècle des Croisades (1095–1188)* (Paris 1889)

N. Elisséeff, *Nur al Din; un Grand Prince Musulman de Syria au Temps des Croisades* (Institut Français de Damas, Damascus 1967)

Encyclopedia of Islam (2nd edition)

H.A.R. Gibb, 'The Armies of Saladin', *Cahiers d'Histoire Egyptienne* III (1951)

W.J. Hamblin, 'Saladin and Muslim Military Theory', in B.Z. Kedar (edit.), *The Horns of Hattin* (Jerusalem and London 1992)

C. Hillenbrand, 'The History of the Jazira, 1100–1250: A Short Introduction', in J. Raby (edit.), *Oxford Studies in Islamic Art*, vol. I (Oxford 1985)

C. Hillenbrand, 'The Islamic World and the Crusades', *The Scottish Journal of Religious Studies* VII (1986)

R.R. Humphreys, *From Saladin to the Mongols: The Ayyubids of Damascus 1193–1260* (Albany NY 1977)

R.S. Humphreys, 'The Emergence of the Mamluk Army', *Studia Islamica* XLV (1977)

D. and W. Paterson, Lathan, 'Horse-archers of Islam', in R. Elgood (edit.), *Islamic Arms and Armour* (London 1979)

B. Lewis, *Islam from the Prophet Muhammad to the Capture of Constantinople, vol. I: Politics and War* (New York 1974)

F. Lokkegaard, 'The Concept of War and Peace in Islam', in B.P. McGuire (edit.), *War and Peace in the Middle Ages* (Copenhagen 1987)

M.C. and D.E.P. Jackson, Lyons, *Saladin: The*

Kitaq al Tiryaq, 'Book of Antidotes', Iraq AD1199. Three men, perhaps a retired amir with two young Turkish retainers, find poisonous snakes in a water jar. (Bibliotheque Nationale, Ms. Ar. 2964, f.5, Paris, France)

Hisn Kayfa (modern Hasankayf) overlooking the river Tigris in south-eastern Turkey where Usama Ibn Munqidh wrote his famous autobiography. He was sixty-nine when he retired so it seems unlikely that he climbed up and down the rock staircase from the Citadel to the river. (Author's photograph)

Right: The early 12th century so-called mihrab *or prayer niche from Gu Kummet, near Sinjar in northern Iraq, was probably a door. It is unusual in being decorated by carved niches including warriors armed with a variety of weapons. This form of decoration was based on Syriac churches and monasteries in northern Iraq, many of which had comparable carvings of saints and monks (Nat. Museum, Baghdad, Iraq)*

Politics of the Holy War (Cambridge 1982)

L.A. Mayer, 'Saracenic Arms and Armour', *Ars Islamica* X (1943)

E. McEwen, (trans.), 'Persian Archery texts: Chapter Eleven of Fakhr-i Mudabbir's Adab al Harb', *The Islamic Quarterly* XVIII (1974)

D.C. Nicolle, 'An Introduction to Arms and Warfare in Classical Islam', in R. Elgood (edit.), *Islamic Arms and Armour* (London 1979)

D.C. Nicolle, *The Arms and Armour of the Crusading Era 1050–1350* (New York 1988)

Nizam al Mulk (trans. H. Darke), *The Book of Government or Rules for Kings: The Siyasat Nama* (London 1960)

V.J. Parry, 'Warfare', in P.M. Holt (edit.), *The Cambridge History of Islam* (Cambridge 1970)

R. Peters, *Jihad in Medieval and Modern Islam* (Leiden 1977)

H. Rabie, 'The Training of the Mamluk Faris', in V.J. Parry and M.E. Yapp (edits.), *War, Technology and Society in the Middle East* (London 1975)

Ibn al Husayn al Sulami (trans. Tosum Bayrak al Jerrahi al Halveti), *The Book of Sufi Chivalry, Futuwwah* (London 1983)

al Tarsusi (trans. A. Boudot-Lamotte), *Contribution à l'Etude de l'Archerie Musulmane* (Institut Français de Damas, Damascus 1968)

al Tarsusi (edit. and trans. C. Cahen), 'Un Traité d'Armurerie composé pour Saladin', *Bulletin d'Etudes Orientales* XII (1947–8)

Usama Ibn Munqidh (trans. P.H. Hitti), *Memoires of an Arab-Syrian Gentleman* (Princeton 1929; reprint Beirut 1964)

A.R. Zaki, 'Military Literature of the Arabs', *Islamic Culture* XXX (1956)

Notes sur les planches en couleur

A1 Cavalier arabe, début 12ème siècle. Il porte un turban sur un casque italien et son corps est protégé par un haubert en cotte de mailles. Comme musulman ses cheveux auraient dû être coupés court mais il est clair que les soldats ne suivaient pas cette injonction. **A2** Détail de la broderie et des motifs de la tunique. **A3** Le haubert en mailles *dir'*. **A3a** Maille avec liens rivetés et poinçonnés. **A3b** Détail du cuir utilisé pour raidir le col. **A4** Casque italien avec décoration en or et bande de bronze sur le rebord. **A5** Marteau de guerre en bronze. Il se peut que le crochet à l'arrière ait été utilisé pour tirer les ennemis de leurs chevaux. **A6** détail d'une épée arabe à lame droite ou *sayf*. **A6a** Epée entièrement assemblée. **A7** Bouclier en bois ou *turs* avec face recouverte de cuir.

B Comme en Europe médiévale, la chasse était une forme réaliste et dangereuse d'entraînement militaire. Usama Ibn Munqidh porte un costume de l'aristocratie syrienne arabe. Sa'dullah al Shaybani, bien qu'il soit un soldat Kurde, porte un casque militaire doublé de fourrure ou *sharbush*. Archers arméniens, bien que chrétiens, s'inscrivaient dans de nombreuses armées musulmanes.

C Durant l'un des fréquents affrontements sur les frontières entre les états musulmans et croisés, Yaqut le Grand fait tomber deux croisés de leur cheval avec un seul coup de lance.

D Matériel de tir à l'arc. **D1** Arc assemblé. **D1a** Quatre points de pression à attacher avec du cuir brut. **D2** Neufs pièces de bois qui constituent le corps de l'arc. **D3** Corne noire. **D4** Morceaux de tendons. **D5** Ecorce de bouleau utilisée comme couverture autour de l'arc. **D6** Cuir brut pour les points de pression **D7** Corde d'arc complète. **D7a** Détail de la corde d'arc. **D7b-D7c** Boucle nouée à chaque extrémité de la corde d'arc. **D8a-D8b** Anneau de pouce en bronze. **D9a-D9c** Anneau de pouce en argent. **D10a-D10b** Anneau de pouce en bronze. **D11a-D11c** Flèche complète montrant l'empennage. **D12a** Corps de flèche scié droit. **D12b** Corps de flèche scié en travers du grain. **D12c** Corps de flèche en chandelle. **D13a-D13b** Pointe de flèche avec lien. **D14a-D14c** Pointes de flèches. **D15** Pointes de flèches en fer. **D16a-D16c** Têtes de flèches avec sifflet en bronze. **D17** Arc composé au repos. **D18** Arc composé chargé. **D19** Main gauche sur l'arc, flèche à la droite de l'arc. **D20** Relâchement primaire. **D21** Relâchement secondaire. **D22** Relâchement tertiaire. **D23** Relâchement méditerranéen. **D24** Chargement au pouce ou relâchement mongolien, avec un anneau de pouce. **D25a-D25c** Variations du chargement au pouce.

E Les archers musulmans utilisaient diverses tactiques, y compris la volée, comme ici. Les chevaux sont immobiles alors que les archers tirent aussi vite qu'ils peuvent dans une 'zone d'offensive' plutôt que sur des individus. Cette tactique essentiellement persane fut mise au point pour combattre les bandits turcs des steppes d'Asie centrale.

Farbtafeln

A1 Arabischer Kavallerist, frühes 12. Jahrhundert. Er trägt einen Turban über dem italienischen Helm und sein Körper wird durch einen Panzerschurz geschützt. Als männlicher Moslem sollte er eigentlich einen kurzen Haarschnitt haben, doch offensichtlich nahmen die Soldaten davon keine Notiz. **A2** Gestickte und aufgedruckte Verzierung der Tunika. **A3** Der *dir'* - Panzerschurz. **A3a** Kettenpanzer mit genieteten und gestanzten Verbindungen. **A3b** Ungegerbtes Leder, das zur Verbrämung des Kragens benutzt wurde. **A4** Italienischer Helm mit goldener Verzierung und Bronzestreifen am Rand. **A5** Kriegshammer aus Bronze, der Haken auf der Rückseite diente unter Umständen dazu, den Feind vom Pferd zu reißen. **A6** Detailansicht eines geradklingigen, arabischen *says*-Schwerts. **A6a** Komplett zusammengebautes Schwert. **A7** Hölzerner *turs*-Schild mit lederbezogener Vorderseite.

B Wie im mittelalterlichen Europa diente die Jagd als wirklichkeitsgetreue und gefährliche Form der Militärübung. Usama Ibn Mundiqh trägt die Kleidung des syrisch-arabischen Adels. Sa'dullah al Shaybani, obgleich kurdischer Soldat, trägt die türkische *sharbush*-Militärmütze mit Pelzfutter. Armenische Bogenschützen traten oft muslimischen Heeren bei, obwohl sie Christen waren.

C Bei einem der haufigen Scharmützel an der Grenze zwischen den Moslem- und den Kreuzritterstaaten reißt Yaqut der Große zwei Kreuzritter mit einem einzigen Lanzenstoß vom Pferd.

D Bogenausrüstung. **D1** Zusammengebauter Bogen und Teilansicht. **D1a** Vier Spannungsspitzen, die mit ungegerbtem Leder zusammengebunden werden. **D2** Neun Holzstücke, die den Rumpf des Bogens bilden. **D3** Schwarzes Horn. **D4** Sehnen. **D5** Die Birkenrinde wird als Hülle um den Bogen gelegt. **D6** Ungegerbtes Leder für die Spannungsspitzen. **D7** Fertige Bogensehne. **D7a** Detailansicht einer Bogensehne. **D7b-D7c** Geknotete Schlaufe an beiden Enden der Bogensehne. **D8a-D8b** Bronzener Daumenring. **D9a-D9c** Silberner Daumenring. **D10a-D10b** Bronzener Daumenring. **D11a-D11c** Fertiger Pfeil mit Befiederung und Kerbe. **D12a** Gerade geschlagener Pfeilschaft. **D12b** Gerstenkorn-Pfeilschaft. **D12c** Kerzenförmiger Pfeilschaft. **D13a-D13b** Pfeilspitze mit Bindung. **D14a-D14c** Pfeilspitzen. **D15** Eiserne Pfeilspitzen. **D16a-D16c** Pfeilspitzen mit bronzenen Pfeifen. **D17** Zusammengesetzter Bogen in Ruhestellung. **D18** Zusammengesetzter, gespannter Bogen. **D19** Linke Hand am Bogen, Pfeil rechts vom Bogen. **D20** Primär-Abschuß. **D21** Sekundär-Abschuß. **D22** Tertiär-Abschuß. **D23** Mittelmeer-Abschuß. **D24** Daumenspannung bzw. Mongolen-Abschuß mit Hilfe eines Daumenrings. **D25a-D25c** Variationen des Daumenzugs.

E Muslimische Bogenschützen bedienten sich einer Reihe von Taktiken, zu denen auch wie hier der Pfeilhagel gehörte. Die Pferde standen still und die

F1 Il porte des vêtements et du matériel turcs. Ses cheveux sont dans un style turc typique avec une longue queue de cheval. Il porte un *Latt*. **F2a-F2d** Vue explosée hypothétique d'un *sharbush*. **F3** détail d'un bouclier. **F4a** Cuirasse lamellaire en fer. **F4b** Vue arrière de la cuirasse. **F4c** Détail de l'intérieur de la veste. **F4d** Vues d'une lame de fer unique. **F4e** Laçage d'une cuirasse lamellaire. **F5a** Extérieur d'un fourreau. **F5b** Intérieur d'un scabbard. **F5c** Section d'un scabbard. **F5d** Couverture en cuir du fourreau. **F5e** Face interne non décorée d'un fourreau. **F5f-h** Point de suspension en bronze. **F5i-k** Vues d'une bouterolle en bronze. **F6a** Lame de sabre. **F6b-c** Deux moitiés de la poignée en bois. **F6d** Rivet supérieur utilisé pour couvreuir la fixations. **F6e-g** Quillons en bronze moulé. **F7** Détail du *latt*, une forme de masse avec une pointe en bronze moulé et un manche en bois. **F8** Bottes de cheval en cuir.

G Les troupes musulmanes avaient un soutien médical bien meilleur que leurs ennemis croisés. Les instruments des croisés étaient basés sur ceux de la Grèce antique, de Rome, d'Inde et de Chine. Les médicaments étaient à base d'extraits de plantes et d'huiles naturelles. Le renouveau de la médecine d'Europe occidentale devait beaucoup à ces docteurs musulmans.

H Harnais de chevaux. **H1** Harnais de cheval arabe mis au point à partir d'un mélange de style bédouins, méditerranéens et iraniens. **H2** Pendant de harnais en bronze. **H3** Attache de bride en bronze. **H4** Lien en bronze en forme de trèfle pour les brides. **H5** Bride complète. **H6** Le châssis en bois de la selle. **H6a** Vue arrière du troussequin **H7** Selle complète avec siège rembourré. **H8** Le harnais des chevaux turcs tribaux, couverture de cheval et pas de selle. **H8a** Le harnais complet. **H8b** Vue supérieure du mors articulé. **H8c** Détail d'une boucle en bronze. **H8d** Médaillon de collier en bronze. **H9** Selle à châssis de bois. **H9a** Troussequin. **H9b** Pommeau. **H9c** Selle de base avec jupe en cuir et rabat en tissu. **H9d** Selle complète avec siège en tissu, panneaux de tissu décoratifs et courroies de poitrine et de reculement. **H9e** Etriers de bronze avec incrustations d'argent. **H9f** Médaillon de bronze percé.

I1 Musulman en costume fonctionnel plutôt que cérémonial. Il porte la première couche de vêtements. **I1a** *Qayah*. **I1b** Pantalon *tubban* **I2**. Chemise ample *qamis* **I3** Pantalons matelassés en laine ou *Sirwal* **I4** Tunique ou manteau en soie ou *Qaba*. **I4a** *Tiraz*. **I4b** Bouton et boucle en tissu pour fermer au cou. **I5** *Qaftan* en laine de style perse. **I6** Lourd *durra'ah* en laine, vêtement pour temps froid. **I7** *Jubah*, manteau en satin doublé de fourrure. **I8a** Calot *quyah* porté sur un chapeau turc en feutre mou ou *qub*. **I8b** *Qalansuwa tawila* ou 'Grand qalansuwa' en tissu sur vannerie ou armature de paille. **I8c** *Qalansuwa shashiya*; Chapeau matelassé couvert de soie. **I8d** Le turban *Imanah*. **I8e** le *immamah adhababa* -plus haut qu'un turban ordinaire. **I8f** Le *imamah muhannak* ou 'turban pendant'. **I9** Épaisses guêtres *ra'n* de tissu solide bordées de cuir. **I10 & 10a** Bottes *khuff* en cuir souple sans guêtres. **I11** Bottes de cheval perses. **I12** Sandales arabes en cuir ou *na'l*. **I13** Chaussures non lacées *Madan*.

J Si un soldat arrivait à survivre aux dangers de la guerre, il pouvait prendre sa retraite dans le respect et peut-être la prospérité. De nombreux soldats en retraite prirent comme métier l'écriture ou l'enseignement alors que d'autres entraînaient les jeunes soldats ou devinrent des marchands.

K1 Guerrier perse avec chapeau en tissu. **K2a-d** Détail de casque. **K3** Reconstitution d'une armure lamellaire perse médiévale. **K3a** Intérieur de la cuirasse. **K3b** Lame de fer simple. **K3c** Petite section de la cuirasse montrant le détail du lacis. **K4** Détail de l'armure doublée de maille ou *Kazadhand* **K4c** Position des bandes *tiraz* autour des manches. **K5a** Petite botte de cheval en cuir souple. **K5b** Lourde guêtre en cuir brut avec rosettes de tissu. **K6** 'hache de cavalerie' en fer avec incrustation d'argent ou *tabarzin*. **K7** Détail d'un bouclier en métal avant le 15ème siècle.

Bogenschützen schießen so schnell sie konnten auf eine "Schußzone", anstatt auf Einzelne zu zielen. Diese eigentlich persische Taktik wurde entwickelt, um mit türkischen Eindringlingen fertig zu werden, die aus den zentralasiatischen Steppen kamen.

F1 Er trägt türkische Kleidung und Ausrüstung, seine Frisur ist typisch türkisch mit einem langen Pferdeschwanz. Er hat eine *latt* bei sich. **F2a-F2d** Hypothetische Darstellung in auseinandergezogener Anordnung eines *sharbush*. **F3** Detailansicht eines Schilds. **F4a** Eiserner Lamellenküraß. **F4b** Rückansicht des Küraß. **F4c** Detailansicht des Inneren der Jacke. **F4d** Ansichten einer einzelnen Eisenschuppe. **F4e** Schnürung eines Lamellenküraß. **F5a** Außenansicht einer Scheide. **F5b** Innenseite einer Scheide. **F5c** Teilansicht einer Scheide. **F5d** Lederhülle für eine Scide. **F5e** Unverzierte Innenseite einer Scheide. **F5f-h** Aufhängung aus Bronze. **F5i-k** Ansichten eines bronzenen Ortbandes. **F6a** Säbelklinge. **F6b-c** Zwei Hälften des Holzgriffes. **F6d** Die obere Niete dient zur Befestigung. **F6e-g** Parierstangen aus Gußbronze. **F7** Detailansicht einer *latt*, einer Form des Streitkolbens mit einem gußbronzenen Kopf und einem hölzernen Schaft. **F8** Reitstiefel aus Leder.

G Die muslimischen Truppen hatten eine viel bessere ärztliche Versorgung als ihre Gegner, die Kreuzritter. Die Instrumente der Ärzte beruhten auf den Vorbildern des antiken Griechenland, Rom, Indien und China. Die Arzneien basierten auf Kräuteraufgüssen und natürlichen Ölen. Der Aufschwung in der westeuropäischen Heilkunst hat diesen muslimischen Ärzten viel zu verdanken.

H Pferdegeschirr. **H1** Arabisches Pferdegeschirr, das aus einer Mischung der beduinischen, mediterranen und der iranischen Macharten entwickelt wurde. **H2** Geschirrgehänge aus Bronze. **H3** Zaumzeug aus Bronze. **H4** Dreiblatt-Riemenverknüpfung aus Bronze. **H5** Komplettes Zaumzeug. **H6** Der hölzerne Sattelrahmen. **H6a** Rückansicht der Hinterzwiesel. **H7** Kompletter Sattel mit gepolstertem Sitz. **H8** Das Pferdegeschirr der türkischen Stämme; Pferdedecke und kein Sattel. **H8a** Das Pferdegeschirr der türkischen Stämme. **H8b** Oberansicht eines scharnierten Bißstücks. **H8c** Detailansicht einer Bronze-Schnalle. **H8d** Lederkummet, das mit Bronze-Medaillons verziert ist. **H9** Sattel mit Holzrahmen. **H9a** Hinterzwiesel. **H9b** Sattelknopf. **H9c** Einfacher Sattel mit Lederschurz und Stofflappen. **H9d** Kompletter Sattel mit Stoffsitz, Schmuckbahnen aus Stoff und Brust- und Umgangsgurten. **H9e** Sporen aus Bronze mit Silbereinlage. **H9f** Gelochtes Bronze-Medaillon.

I1 Moslem in Kleidung, die eher funktional als zeremoniell ist. Er trägt die erste Kleidungsschicht. **I1a** *qayah*. **I1b** *Tubban*-Unterhosen. **I2** Loses *qamis*-Hemd. **I3** Wattierte *Sirwal*-Hosen. **I4** *Qaba*-Seidentunika bzw. Mantel. **I4a** *Tiraz*. **I4b** Stopfknopf und Schlaufe als Halsverschluß. **I5** Wollener *qaftan* im persischen Stil. **I6** Schwerer, wollener *durra'ah* - ein Kleidungsstück für kaltes Wetter. **I7** *Jubah*-Mantel aus pelzgefüttertem Satin. **I8a** *Quyah*-Käppchen, das über der türkischen *qub*-Mütze aus weichem Filz getragen wurde. **I8b** *Qalansuwa tawila* oder aus Stoff über Flechtwerk- bzw. Strohrahmen. **I8c** *Qalansuwa shashiya*; Wattierter Hut, mit Seide bezogen. **I8d** Der *Imamah*-Turban. **I8e** Der *immamah adhahaba* - höher als der gewöhnliche Turban. **I8f** Der *imamah_muhannak* bzw. "Hänge-Turban". **I9** Dicke *ra'n*-Gamaschen aus festem Stoff, mit Leder eingesäumt. **I10 & I10a** *Khuff*-Stiefel aus weichem Leder ohne Gamaschen. **I11** Persische Reitstiefel. **I12** Arabische *na'l*-Ledersandalen. **I13** *Madan*-Slipper.

J Gelang es einem Soldaten, den Gefahren des Krieges zu entrinnen, so konnte er sich in geachteter Stellung und vielleicht sogar im Wohlstand zur Ruhe setzen. Viele der pensionierten Soldaten versuchten sich als Schriftsteller oder Lehrer, andere bildeten junge Soldaten aus oder wurden Händler.

K1 Persischer Krieger mit Stoffmütze über dem Helm. **K2a-d** Detailansicht eines Helms. **K3** Rekonstruktion eines mittelalterlichen, persischen Lamellenpanzers. **K3a** Innenseite des Küraß. **K3b** Einzelne Eisenschuppe. **K3c** Ausschnitt des Küraß mit Detailansicht der Schnürung. **K4** Detailansicht der *Kazaghand*-Rüstung mit Kettenpanzer im Innern. **K4c** Anordnung der *tiraz*-Bänder um die Ärmel. **K5a** Kleiner Reitstiefel aus weichem Leder. **K5b** Feste Gamaschen aus ungegerbtem Leder mit Stoffrosetten. **K6** Eiserne *tabarzin*-"Kavallerieaxt" mit Silbereinlage. **K7** Detailansicht eines Metallschilds vor dem 15. Jahrhundert.